LANDMARKS OF WORLD LITERATURE

Milton

Paradise Lost

LANDMARKS OF WORLD LITERATURE
Second Editions

MILTON

Paradise Lost

DAVID LOEWENSTEIN

Department of English, University of Wisconsin, Madison

 CAMBRIDGE
UNIVERSITY PRESS

PUBLISHED BY THE PRESS SYNDICATE OF THE UNIVERSITY OF CAMBRIDGE
The Pitt Building, Trumpington Street, Cambridge CB2 1RP, United Kingdom

CAMBRIDGE UNIVERSITY PRESS
The Edinburgh Building, Cambridge, CB2 2RU, UK
40 West 20th Street, New York, NY 10011–4211, USA
477 Williamstown Road, Port Melbourne, VIC 3207, Australia
Ruiz de Alarcón 13, 28014 Madrid, Spain
Dock House, The Waterfront, Cape Town 8001, South Africa

http://www.cambridge.org

First published 1993, second edition 2004

Printed in the United Kingdom at the University Press, Cambridge

Typeface Photina 10/12 pt.   *System* LaTeX 2_ε [TB]

A catalogue record for this book is available from the British Library

ISBN 0 521 83212 8 hardback
ISBN 0 521 53979 X paperback

For Stella Amadea

The world is all before you . . .

Contents

Contents

Preface and note on abbreviations

Milton's friend and contemporary, the poet Andrew Marvell, was struck by the sheer audacity and boldness of *Paradise Lost*:

> When I beheld the Poet blind, yet bold,
> In slender Book his vast Design unfold,
> *Messiah* Crown'd, God's Reconcil'd Decree,
> Rebelling Angels, the Forbidden Tree
> Heav'n, Hell, Earth, Chaos, All; the Argument
> Held me a while misdoubting his Intent,
> That he would ruin (for I saw him strong)
> The sacred Truths to Fable and old Song.

These commendatory lines from Marvell's "On Mr. Milton's *Paradise Lost*" (1674) capture well the extraordinary cosmic scope of Milton's sublime poem and the ambition of its blind, prophetic author. This "Mighty Poet" would (as Marvell observes later) soar "above human flight" as he dares to give new imaginative expression to divine truth – even at the risk of sacrificing it to fable – in an epic poem fully rivalling its precursors, as well as the very Bible itself. A sensitive and astute reader of Milton's *Paradise Lost*, Marvell recognized that it was a "landmark" of sorts, for no other poem in Milton's age had attempted to do so much by lifting, in the words of the archangel Raphael, "Human imagination to such highth / Of Godlike Power" (*PL* 6.300–1). The "vast Design" of *Paradise Lost* combined epic form and sacred themes to create a poetic composition entirely new. Along with Marvell, the reader of *Paradise Lost* today might well continue to respond to this most ambitious and perilous poetic enterprise with a sense of wonder, admiration, and apprehension: "At once delight and horror on us seize" – so Marvell later in the same poem sums up his response. In treating *Paradise Lost* as a "landmark" of world literature and in attempting to define major aspects of this visionary poem for the non-specialist reader, I have tried to convey something of Milton's imaginative daring and creative originality, qualities immediately apparent to one of its most perceptive contemporary readers.

Quotations from Milton's poetry are taken from Merritt Y. Hughes's edition, *John Milton: Complete Poetry and Major Prose* (Indianapolis, 1957), while Milton's prose is cited from the Yale edition of *The Complete Prose Works of John Milton*, gen. ed. Don M. Wolfe, 8 vols. (New Haven, 1953–82). The Yale edition of the prose is cited in my text as YP, followed by the volume and page number. Biblical citations are from the Authorized (King James) Version.

Finally, I would like to thank those individuals who offered valuable critical advice as I was preparing this book: Katharina Brett, Thomas Corns, Robin Grey, Michael Silk, Peter Stern, Kevin Taylor, James G. Turner, and Andrew Weiner. I am saddened, however, that Peter Stern did not live to see its completion, since he was, in Miltonic terms, the begetter and prime cause of the series *Landmarks of World Literature*. I can only hope that this book measures up to the exacting standards he set as general editor.

For the new edition of this book, I have revised and updated the guide to further reading and made some minor corrections in the main text.

Chronology

Year	Milton's life and significant works	Historical and cultural events
1608	Born in Bread Street, Cheapside, London on December 9; his father was a scrivener, musician, and composer.	
1609		Shakespeare, *Sonnets*; Jonson, *Epicoene* and *The Masque of Queens*. Clarendon born. Suckling born.
1610		Galileo reports on his telescopic observation of the heavens. Henry IV of France assassinated. Jonson, *The Alchemist*; Shakespeare, *The Winter's Tale* (?).
1611		Shakespeare, *The Tempest*; King James Bible; Donne, *The First Anniversary*.
1612		Death of Henry, prince of Wales. Donne, *The Second Anniversary*.
1613		Galileo, *Letters on Sunspots*. Crashaw born (c. 1613). La Rochefoucauld born.
1614		Raleigh, *The History of the World*; Jonson, *Bartholomew Fair*; Webster, *The Duchess of Malfi*.
1616		Ben Jonson, *Works*; James I, *Works*; Chapman's *Whole Works of Homer*. Death of Shakespeare and Cervantes.

(cont.)

	Milton's life and significant works	Historical and cultural events
1618		Bacon appointed Lord Chancellor; Raleigh executed. Thirty Years War starts (to 1648). Cowley and Lovelace born.
1619		Kepler, *De harmonice mundi*.
1620	Enters St. Paul's school, London, where he receives a humanist education.	Religious migration of the Pilgrim Fathers to the New World. Bacon, *Novum Organum*. John Evelyn born.
1621		Donne appointed Dean of St. Paul's. Bacon impeached. Burton, *Anatomy of Melancholy*. Marvell and Henry Vaughan born. La Fontaine born.
1622		Molière born.
1623		Shakespeare's First Folio. Pascal born. Death of William Byrd.
1624		George Fox, founder of the Quakers, born.
1625	Admitted to Christ's College, Cambridge (February 12).	Death of James I; accession of Charles I and marriage to Henrietta Maria of France.
1626		Death of Bacon.
1628		Buckingham assassinated. Harvey's work on the circulation of the blood published. Bunyan born.
1629	Takes BA degree. Composes ode *On the Morning of Christ's Nativity*.	Charles I dissolves Parliament, governing without it until 1640.

Year		
1630		Prince Charles (future Charles II) born. Great Migration to New England begins.
1631		Death of Donne and Drayton. Dryden born.
1632	Receives MA. Begins period of "studious retirement" at parents' residence in Hammersmith; extensive reading in history and politics.	Galileo, *Dialogue on the Two Principal World Systems*. Van Dyck settles in England. Wren, Locke, and Spinoza born.
1633		William Laud becomes Archbishop of Canterbury. Herbert, *The Temple*; Donne, *Poems*. Death of Herbert. Pepys born.
1634	Performance of *A Mask* (*Comus*) at Ludlow Castle, September 29.	Carew's masque *Coelum Britannicum*.
1635	Residence at Horton, Buckinghamshire; continues private studies.	
1637	Writes *Lycidas* (published in 1638). *Comus* published.	Descartes, *Discourse on Method*. Corneille, *Le Cid*. Death of Jonson.
1638	Begins continental tour in April: meets important patrons, scholars, and intellectuals in France and Italy including Hugo Grotius (famous Dutch writer, theologian, and jurist) and Galileo.	
1639	Visits theologian John Diodati in Geneva; returns to England in July. Writes *Epitaphium Damonis* to commemorate the death of his friend Charles Diodati.	First Bishops' War against Scotland. Racine born.

(*cont.*)

	Milton's life and significant works	Historical and cultural events
1640	Begins tutoring nephews in London.	Short Parliament; Second Bishops' War; Long Parliament meets; Strafford and Laud impeached; censorship breaks down. Aphra Behn born. Death of Rubens.
1641	Begins pamphleteering against episcopacy: *Of Reformation, Of Prelatical Episcopacy, Animadversions* published.	Execution of Strafford; Irish Rebellion; Grand Remonstrance. Death of Van Dyck.
1642	*The Reason of Church-Government, An Apology for Smectymnuus* published. Marries Mary Powell (July?) of a Royalist family; she returns to her family (in August?).	Outbreak of Civil War; Battle of Edgehill. Death of Galileo. Theaters closed. Newton born.
1643	*The Doctrine and Discipline of Divorce* published.	The Westminster Assembly of Divines; Solemn League and Covenant. Louis XIV becomes king of France. Browne, *Religio Medici*.
1644	*Of Education, The Judgement of Martin Bucer, Concerning Divorce,* and *Areopagitica* published.	Battle of Marston Moor.
1645	Mary Powell Milton returns. Final divorce tracts, *Tetrachordon* and *Colasterion,* published. *Poems of Mr. John Milton, Both English and Latin* registered for publication (published January 1646).	Laud executed; the New Model Army formed: victory at Naseby.

Year		
1646	Milton's daughter Anne born (July).	Charles I surrenders to the Scots; end of First Civil War; episcopacy abolished. Crashaw, *Steps to the Temple*. Browne, *Pseudodoxia Epidemica*.
1647	Death of Milton's father.	Scots hand Charles over to the English; Charles arrested. The Levellers' *Agreement of the People*; the Putney Debates. King escapes. Rochester born.
1648	Milton's daughter Mary born (October).	Second Civil War; Pride purges Parliament. Peace of Westphalia ends Thirty Years War. Herrick, *Hesperides*.
1649	*The Tenure of Kings and Magistrates* (February) and *Eikonoklastes* (October) published. Appointed Secretary for Foreign Tongues by the Council of State (March).	Trial and execution of Charles I (January); abolition of monarchy and House of Lords; Commonwealth declared. Cromwell crushes Irish Rebellion. Death of Crashaw.
1650		Marvell's "Horatian Ode"; Vaughan, *Silex Scintillans* (*The Fiery Flint*). Death of Descartes.
1650–2		Cromwell conquers Scotland (battles of Dunbar and Worcester).
1651	*Pro Populo Anglicano Defensio* (*First Defense*) published. Third child, John, born (March).	Hobbes, *Leviathan*.
1652	Becomes totally blind by February. Daughter Deborah born (May). Death of Mary Powell Milton (May) and son John (June).	Anglo-Dutch War (to 1654). Gerrard Winstanley, *The Law of Freedom in a Platform*. Death of Inigo Jones.

(cont.)

(cont.)

	Milton's life and significant works	Historical and cultural events
1653		Rump Parliament dissolved; Cromwell becomes Lord Protector.
1654	*Pro Populo Anglicano Defensio Secunda (Second Defense)* published.	First Protectorate Parliament.
1655	*Pro Se Defensio (Defense of Himself)* published.	War with Spain (to 1659). Fanshawe's translation of Camoens's epic *The Lusiads*.
1656	Marries Katherine Woodcock.	Harrington, *Commonwealth of Oceana.*
1657		Death of the Leveller John Lilburne. Cromwell refuses the crown.
1658	Death of Katherine Woodcock Milton and their infant daughter Katherine. Begins *Paradise Lost.*	Death of Cromwell; son Richard becomes Lord Protector. Browne, *Urn Burial* and *The Garden of Cyrus.*
1659	*A Treatise of Civil Power in Ecclesiastical Causes* and *Considerations Touching the Likeliest Means to Remove Hirelings out of the Church* published.	Collapse of Richard Cromwell's Protectorate; the Rump Parliament and Commonwealth restored. Purcell born.
1660	*The Ready and Easy Way to Establish a Free Commonwealth* (first edition published in February; revised and enlarged edition appears in early April). Milton goes into hiding. Arrested and imprisoned (October?); freed on December 15, with the help of Andrew Marvell and Sir William Davenant.	Stuart monarchy restored (May): Charles II as king; House of Lords restored. Pepys begins his diary. Theaters reopen. Royal Society founded. Dryden, *Astraea Redux.* Death of Velasquez.

Year	Milton	Historical and literary events
1661		In France, Louis XIV assumes full powers.
1662		The Licensing Act. The Act of Uniformity. Death of Henry Lawes and Pascal.
1663	Marries Elizabeth Minshull.	Butler, *Hudibras*.
1665		Outbreak of the Great Plague. Second Anglo-Dutch War (to 1667). Hooke, *Micrographia*.
1666		The Great Fire of London. Bunyan, *Grace Abounding to the Chief of Sinners*. Molière, *Le Misanthrope*.
1667	*Paradise Lost* published in ten books.	Fall of Clarendon. Dryden, *Annus Mirabilis*. Sprat, *History of the Royal Society*. Swift born.
1668		Dryden becomes Poet Laureate.
1669	*Accidence Commenced Grammar* published.	Death of Rembrandt. Molière, *Tartuffe* (final version).
1670	*The History of Britain* published.	Treaty of Dover signed with France. Congreve born.
1671	*Paradise Regained* and *Samson Agonistes* published together.	
1672	*Art of Logic* published.	Third Anglo-Dutch War (to 1674).
1673	*Of True Religion, Heresy, Schism, and Toleration* (his last prose tract) published. Second and enlarged edition of *Poems* published.	The First Test Act. Wren begins St. Paul's Cathedral. Death of Molière.
1674	Second edition of *Paradise Lost* (in twelve books) published. Death (probably on November 8) "in a fit of the gout"; buried on November 12 in St. Giles, Cripplegate.	Death of Herrick, Traherne, and Clarendon.

The chronology of events in *Paradise Lost*

Chapter 1

Paradise Lost in Milton's career and age

1 "Long choosing, and beginning late"

The sublime prophetic poem which so impressed Andrew Marvell in the lines quoted in the preface to this volume was not the work of a youthful poet. By the time Milton wrote *Paradise Lost*, he was a blind man in his fifties, disappointed with the failures of church and state reformation, and yet aspiring to write a new kind of epic poem – one focusing on sacred truths and attempting, after the collapse of the English Revolution, to "assert Eternal Providence, / And justify the ways of God to men" (1.25–6). Although he had published his youthful *Poems* (1645–6) and had achieved considerable prominence as a controversial pamphleteer, he had still not written anything in verse nearly as ambitious nor as comprehensive as *Paradise Lost*. Yet Milton's earlier career can be seen as essential preparation for this great visionary project whose sacred subject and ambitious form he considered over many years. We need to begin, then, by addressing the literary choices and vocational issues that led to the composition of Milton's sublime epic.

We know that Milton was indeed "long choosing, and beginning late" in the sacred subject of his "Heroic Song": so he tells us in the invocation to Book 9 of his poem. *Paradise Lost* was probably written between 1658 and 1663, a transitional period when he was completing much of his long career as a political pamphleteer and passionately opposing the Stuart Restoration which occurred in 1660. Milton's early biographer and nephew, Edward Phillips, told John Aubrey (another biographer) that Milton "began about 2 years before the King came in, and finished about 3 years after the King's Restoration" (*Early Lives*, p. 13). Phillips noted, however, that several years before the poem was begun (Aubrey suggests fifteen or sixteen years before), his uncle showed him lines from Satan's soliloquy on Mt. Niphates (4.32–41), then considered "the very beginning" of a tragedy (*Early Lives*, p. 72). Milton composed and dictated as many as forty lines of *Paradise Lost* during the winter nights and mornings – he refers to the Muse's "nightly visitation" in his poem (*PL* 9.22; cf. 7.28–30) – which he would then cut down to half that number; Phillips would come to visit on occasion to look over the manuscript and correct spelling and punctuation. Milton thus seems to have taken about "4 or 5 years" to write the poem (so Aubrey recorded from Phillips) which Thomas Ellwood, one of Milton's young Quaker friends and former students, claims to have seen completed in 1665. Delayed by the Great Plague of 1665 and the Great Fire of 1666, the publication of *Paradise Lost* finally occurred in 1667. It was first published in ten books and reissued in 1668 and 1669 with the addition of the prose Arguments and a defensive note on verse explaining why the poem does not rhyme. It was then published in 1674 in twelve books, a modified design more closely following Virgil's epic.

Although in terms of structure Milton chose to follow Virgil, he had also chosen to write an eternal epic on a sacred theme – not an epic focusing on older imperialistic themes (like the *Aeneid*) or a nationalistic poem celebrating a prominent leader such as Oliver Cromwell, whose achievements in the English Revolution Milton had lavishly praised in his Latin pamphlet, *Defensio Secunda* (1654). Nor did he choose to celebrate an earthly monarch such as King Arthur from legendary British history, the subject matter of Spenser's "historicall fiction," *The Faerie Queene*. The sublime Protestant epic of its age, *Paradise Lost* fully rivals and supersedes its classical and European precursors – a poem written by a poet inwardly illuminated by the spirit of the Bible and the light of God. Yet why did the ambitious poet finally decide against writing a nationalistic epic in favor of composing a sacred one?

From early in his career, Milton, always highly self-conscious about his literary vocation and precocious in his poetic enterprises, had planned to write a great heroic poem on an exalted subject. His early poems register this ambition: in "At a Vacation Exercise in the College" (1628) Milton expresses his wish to devote himself to "some graver subject" in English and to sing (in the manner of Homer) "of Kings and Queens and *Heroes* old, / Such as the wise *Demodocus* once told." And in *Elegy VI* (1629) he envisioned writing a poem concerning "wars and heaven under Jupiter in his prime, and pious heroes, and chieftains half-divine"; in that early piece, moreover, Milton stresses the sacrifices which the sacerdotal poet, conducting a fastidious and unblemished life, must make in order to write serious heroic verse. In *Mansus* and *Epitaphium Damonis* (both of 1639), Milton clearly has in mind for his subject the heroic King Arthur and his Round Table, as well as legendary British history from the time of the Trojan settlement under Brutus, great-grandson of Aeneas and (according to medieval British chroniclers) founder of Britain and New Troy (later London). Other possibilities for subjects from British and Scottish history are recorded in the Trinity College, Cambridge Manuscript (*c.* 1639–42); Milton's notes and drafts from the early 1640s also mention numerous Biblical subjects, including four drafts of a projected tragic drama on the Fall of man, two of them entitled "Paradise Lost" and "Adam unparadiz'd." Indeed, Edward Phillips himself observes that the subject of *Paradise Lost* was "first designed a Tragedy" (*Early Lives*, p. 72). The fact that Milton first thought of the Fall in dramatic and tragic terms is itself significant: though an epic, *Paradise Lost* contains important elements of tragedy, as the invocation to Book 9 makes clear, when Milton indicates that now – as he is about to begin the "Sad task" of relating the drama of mankind's disobedience and fall – he "must change" his "Notes to Tragic" (13, 5–6).

Still, in the early 1640s Milton had not firmly made up his mind about the form or subject of his "Heroic Song." In his antiprelatical pamphlet, *The Reason of Church-Government* (1642), he explored further his poetic and prophetic ambitions, envisioning himself as a national poet and political reformer, "an interpreter & relater of the best and sagest things among mine own Citizens throughout this Iland in the mother dialect" (YP 1:811–12). Milton considered three forms for his poetic project "doctrinal and exemplary to a Nation": the long epic modeled on the poems of Homer, Virgil, and Tasso; the brief epic modeled on the Book of Job; and Greek tragedy, with Sophocles and Euripides as his chief models. (Milton would later write a brief epic in *Paradise Regained* and model his drama based on the Book of Judges, *Samson Agonistes*, on Greek tragedy.)

Church-Government contains much that is pertinent to understanding Milton's poetic development and sense of "inward prompting": besides expressing his national literary aspirations, it expresses his Renaissance ambition to "leave something so written to aftertimes, as they should not willingly let it die" (YP 1:810); it highlights his sense of the Bible as poetic (with its "frequent songs"); and it articulates his sense of the visionary power of the gifted poet who, purified and inspired like the prophet of Isaiah 6:6, might use his God-given talents to sing "in glorious and lofty Hymns . . . Gods Almightinesse, and what he works" (YP 1:817) – as *Paradise Lost* itself does when, for example, the poet's voice joins the angelic song of Book 3 (410–15). Yet Milton's pamphlet of 1642, however revealing about his early ambitions and literary sensibility, does not settle on a subject for Milton's prophetic work, whatever form it might finally take.

Sometime after 1639 and before he began writing *Paradise Lost*, Milton rejected the idea of writing an Arthuriad. Indeed, by the time Milton is working on the *History of Britain* (begun before March 1649 and resumed after 1655), he expresses considerable skepticism about the story from legendary history: "who *Arthur* was, and whether ever any such reign'd in *Britain*, hath bin doubted heertofore, and may again with good reason" (YP 5:164). There were good reasons for Milton turning away from this national myth; for one thing, there was increasing skepticism in his age about the old fables of legendary British history and a preference instead for the truths and authority of sacred history. Furthermore, the story of King Arthur had been associated with royal propaganda from Tudor to Stuart times (whose monarchs claimed to be derived from him), and the revolutionary writer who zealously challenged Stuart power and authority during the 1640s and 1650s was unlikely to choose such a myth – especially one requiring him to celebrate an earthly king and court – for his great poem.

So Milton, increasingly disenchanted with national politics, settled instead on a more universal theme – the story of Adam and Eve and the fall of humankind. Milton's Biblical subject was not only historically sound, but international in its interest. The Bible, after all, was the key text in the lives of Protestants, and Milton chose to base his poem about origins and beginnings on the first chapters of its first book, whose terse details *Paradise Lost* so brilliantly elaborates.

Moreover, rather than choosing a real or legendary national hero or an earthly monarch to place at the center of his epic, Milton chose instead Adam and Eve, mythic figures not bound to any one national history or heritage. And in choosing to relate the original story of the Fall in the form of the long epic, Milton chose what was by far the most ambitious and comprehensive of all literary genres in the Renaissance, a form whose name, we shall see (section 7), he would dare to raise to new and exciting heights.

In order to ready himself for his major poetic achievement, Milton prepared himself through many years of "labour and intent study" (YP 1:810). He received a humanist education, with its emphasis on classical culture and texts, at St. Paul's School, which he entered in 1620; and from 1625 to 1632 he continued his education at Christ's College, Cambridge, whose scholastic and narrow curriculum he found unsatisfactory. At Cambridge, where according to Phillips Milton was admired for his "extraordinary Wit and Reading" (*Early Lives*, p. 54), he engaged in academic disputations or Prolusions. He argued, for example, whether learning makes men happier than does ignorance, and this rhetorical training would later contribute to his versatile polemical skills as a prose writer and to the impressive rhetorical speeches and debates of *Paradise Lost*. Following Cambridge, he began a period of studious retirement and additional preparation (thanks to his father's continuing financial support), which enabled him to read widely in Greek, Latin, and Italian authors, and to deepen his knowledge of history, politics, and ecclesiastical matters. A subsequent continental tour (1638–39) enabled Milton to meet Hugo Grotius and the blind and imprisoned Galileo, the only contemporary, besides Milton himself, mentioned in *Paradise Lost*. Milton's warm reception by poets, patrons and intellectuals in private Florentine humanist academies reinforced his commitment to humanist values, as well as his keen sense of literary vocation. Upon returning to England until the time he began to serve the state as Secretary for Foreign Tongues in 1649, he worked as a private tutor, providing his nephews and other students with the sort of demanding education he believed the serious poet himself must possess – "a thorough knowledge of all the arts and sciences" (*Prolusion VII*, YP 1:288–9). Milton's pamphlet, *Of Education* (1644), records the rigorous scheme of education he advocated, including his interest in educational reform and the new empiricism, encouraged in his age by such figures as Francis Bacon and Samuel Hartlib (the notable Protestant reformer to whom the tract is addressed). It should not surprise us, then, to find that *Paradise Lost* itself explores a number of important pedagogical relationships – between the poet and his muse ("Instruct me, for Thou know'st," 1.19), between Adam and the angel Raphael in Books 5–8, and, after the Fall, between Adam and Michael, who instructs his pupil in the trying lessons of history.

Moreover, the poet who was "long choosing, and beginning late" in his sacred subject always possessed a strong sense of his future-oriented literary vocation and a fascination with his own evolving genius, or what Wordsworth would call the "growth of a poet's mind." Highly ambitious, Milton was self-conscious about his precociousness and virtuosity as a poet from an early age. At the age of twenty-one he composed his ode *On the Morning of Christ's Nativity* (1629), a prophetic poem whose complicated time scheme and cosmic vision range from the Creation to the Apocalypse (as does *Paradise Lost*), and a work which envisions the banishing of pagan oracles and idols with the advent of Christ, a particularly Protestant theme. It is at the beginning of this poem of vocational anticipation that Milton self-consciously announces his calling as a sacred poet, as he imagines himself arriving at the nativity scene before the wise men in order to present his "humble ode":

> Have thou the honor first, thy Lord to greet,
>   And join thy voice unto the Angel Choir,
> From out his secret Altar toucht with hallow'd fire.

The allusion to Isaiah 6:6, the same Biblical passage Milton later refers to in *Church-Government*, underscores the aspiring Milton's sense of prophetic authority, a characteristic of his literary vocation that would distinguish his poetry and prose from this point on. Furthermore, Milton would continue to insert himself dramatically into his literary creations – as he does, for example, in *Lycidas*, throughout his prose, and in the proems to Books 1, 3, 7, and 9 of *Paradise Lost* – so that the drama of vocation itself would become a central focus of his works.

When he published his 1645 *Poems* – the volume of English and Latin verses displaying his diverse and precocious literary development in the 1620s and 1630s – Milton included on the title page a telling motto from Virgil's seventh Eclogue: "Crown my brow with foxglove lest an evil tongue harm the destined poet [*Baccare frontem / Cingite, ne vati noceat mala lingua futuro*]." The passage underscores yet once more his sense of the prophetic poet as sacred and chosen, a gifted writer whose work and self were already worthy of protection from rude ears and hostile tongues. And in *Ad Patrem*, the Latin poem in which he justified his poetic vocation to his father (who hoped his gifted son would pursue more gainful employment), Milton insists that cruel calumny cannot harm the ambitious and fame-oriented youthful poet ("I shall no longer mingle unknown with the dull rabble") who walks "far from the sight of profane eyes" and produces divine poetry, with its mark of Promethean fire (Hughes, pp. 82–6). Throughout his career, Milton not only presented himself as leading a "pure and honorable life" (*Second Defense*, YP 4:611), but defined his role as a poet and prophet in distinctly aesthetic terms, envisioning a self transformed into a work of art: he who would hope "to write well hereafter in laudable things," Milton observed in one of his early pamphlets, must himself be "a true Poem, that is, a composition, and patterne of the best and honourablest things" (*An Apology for Smectymnuus*, YP 1:890). And so from early in his career, the ambitious and self-conscious poet not only believed that he must make himself into "a true Poem", but that as a poet-prophet "separate to God" (*Samson*, 31) he was destined to accomplish extraordinary things.

2 *Lycidas*

The most profound and moving of Milton's early explorations of his vocation as poet-prophet occurs in his pastoral elegy *Lycidas* (1637), a poem whose remarkable achievements look forward, in a number of ways, to *Paradise Lost*; consequently some of its important features deserve a brief account here. Milton laments the untimely death of Edward King, one of Milton's promising contemporaries at Christ's College, Cambridge, who had drowned in the Irish Seas "ere his prime" (8). The poem, however, becomes primarily an occasion to explore Milton's own keen sense of vocational ambitions and uncertainties, especially as he mourns a youthful scholar-poet and model pastor suddenly and arbitrarily cut down, as was King or the "Young *Lycidas*" (9) in the poem's fiction. While Milton responds with pain, horror, and anger to this premature death and incomplete life, and while he laments the vulnerability of the aspiring poet who scorns delights and labors "with uncessant care" in his "homely slighted Shepherd's trade" (64–5), he nevertheless hopes that "some gentle Muse" might "favor [his] destin'd Urn" (19–20). Placing himself in a long line of ancient and Renaissance pastoralists (including Theocritus, Virgil, Spenser, among others), Milton creates an idyllic pastoral world, the rustic innocence of which is now shattered by the death of Lycidas (whose name recalls the shepherd poet in Virgil's ninth Eclogue):

> We drove afield, and both together heard
> What time the Gray-fly winds her sultry horn,
> Batt'ning our flocks with the fresh dews of night . . .   (27–9)

Milton nostalgically imagines their ideal life in Cambridge in terms of a pastoral day, with the young poets themselves as shepherds, but then punctures the illusion, as he registers the pain of losing this paradise: "But O the heavy change, now thou art gone, / Now thou art gone, and never must return!" (37–8). Indeed, much of the poem vacillates between the poet's attempts to find comfort in the pastoral fiction and his hard realization that the pastoral is nothing more than fiction that can barely console his feelings of anxiety and anguish at the unexplained death of young Lycidas: "Let our frail thoughts dally with false surmise" (153), he observes after the beautiful flower passage, only to go on to express his shock – "Ay me!" (154) – at the thought that Lycidas's bones, wherever they may be, have no "Laureate Hearse" (151) on which to strew the flowers. Nor is there a grave – only a "wat'ry bier" (12). *Lycidas* is an emotionally jagged poem, a poem of weltering moods: feelings of pain, loss, anger, and consolation coexist in this powerful meditation on the vulnerability of the poet and his vocation. Even the mythic poet Orpheus found no protection when he was torn apart by the Thracian women: his mother Calliope – "The Muse herself" (58) – Milton painfully observes could not save her son, a poignant vision of dismemberment that the solitary poet would later recall in *Paradise Lost* (7.32–7). And, indeed, if the mythic Orpheus found no protection, why should the young and unknown Milton expect it?

Like the invocations to *Paradise Lost*, where Milton self-consciously explores his poetic authority and ambitions, *Lycidas* is concerned with the self-projection of the ambitious poet and the drama of his composition:

> Yet once more, O ye Laurels, and once more
> Ye Myrtles brown, with Ivy never sere,
> I come to pluck your Berries harsh and crude . . .   (1–3)

Milton begins by announcing his unreadiness, his unripeness as a poet, despite his need to participate in the emotional ritual of mourning a fellow poet's death: both the poet and Lycidas, in their own ways, are untimely. In fact, Milton had written no poetry since *Comus* (1634), his occasional and highly personal entertainment dramatizing the trials and glamor of chaste youthfulness while honoring the earl of Bridgewater's family. Now, reluctantly and with a sense of uncertainty, he takes up his pen again: indeed, one of the tensions of Milton's early career is the conflict between his sense of unripeness (see also the sonnet, "How soon hath time," for his anxious sense of belatedness) and his sense of precociousness as a poet; concerned about his literary tardiness (he refers to his "slow-endeavoring art" in his epitaph on Shakespeare), Milton also feared beginning prematurely. In *Lycidas*, Milton makes that anxiety about his poetic readiness one of the principal themes of his poem. By the end – after the painful, emotionally wrenching process of mourning and consolation has finished – the more mature, future-oriented pastoralist now warbles his lay "With eager thought" (189), no longer uncertain as he was at the outset.

Milton's unsettling meditation on vocational themes generates one of the most distinctive features of *Lycidas*: its passionate and angry prophetic voice. We have noted that his Nativity Ode inaugurated the young Milton's prophetic stance and career; but here, nearly eight years later, Milton's prophetic voice takes on a much more vehement, politically engaged dimension that anticipates his prose polemics and great poems. Even the poem's opening, "Yet once more," alludes to the promise of apocalyptic judgement in Hebrews 12:26–7. The death of one of the nation's young model pastors struck a deep chord in Milton (even though Milton seems not to have been King's close friend), prompting, through his use of the pastoral code, the poem's impassioned religious and political criticism. As if to make the political dimension of the poem more explicit, Milton added a telling headnote to *Lycidas* when he published his 1645 *Poems*: "by occasion" his prophetic poem "foretells the ruin of our corrupted Clergy then in their height." Milton, who had himself considered an ecclesiastical career, felt "Church-outed by the Prelats," as he later noted in *Church-Government* (YP 1:823), and *Lycidas*, especially through the fiery apocalyptic voice of St. Peter, registers his profound disillusionment with the corrupt Anglican clergy. The inexplicable death of Lycidas seems even more unjust when the present clergy – with their "Blind mouths" (suggesting their rapacity and gluttony) – are such bad shepherds, their sermons merely fashionable and superficial exercises ("lean and flashy songs"), the work of bad artists (they grate on "scrannel Pipes of wretched straw") that cannot feed or satisfy their Christian flock (119, 123, 124). Milton's criticisms recall a Biblical text such as Ezekiel 34:2 ("Woe *be* to the shepherds of Israel that do feed themselves! should not the shepherds feed the flocks?"), giving Biblical pastoral a radical Protestant inflection as he builds up to the climactic vision of judgement in which "that two-handed engine at the door / Stands ready to smite once, and smite no more" (130–1). This ominous passage of promised retribution, a famous crux in Milton criticism (it seems to refer to, among other things, the "Two massy Keys" [110] of St. Peter earlier in the poem, and to the sharp two-edged sword issuing out of the apocalyptic Christ's mouth in Rev. 1:16 and 19:15), looks forward to the fierce "two-handed" sword of the warrior angel Michael which "smites" Satan and his rebel forces in *Paradise Lost*'s apocalyptic battle in heaven for the territory of God (see 6.251ff.).

Lycidas is a poem that essentially uses a classical form and gives it, through the language of religious prophecy and anticipation, a radical Christian meaning – one that is "of a higher mood" (87) than its classical tradition. (Its penultimate section of consolation, beginning "Weep no more" [165], is explicitly Christian in emphasis as it alludes to such scriptural passages as Rev. 7:17 and 21:4, where the heavenly voice says that "God shall wipe away all tears," as well as to the marriage song of the Lamb in Rev. 19.) In that sense, too, *Lycidas* anticipates *Paradise Lost*, a poem that takes the highest classical form – the epic – and fundamentally transforms it, so that it suits Milton's ambitious prophetic Protestant aim to "justify the ways of God to men." Milton's relation to his classical contexts and genres is never simple: in his earlier prophetic Nativity Ode, where he envisions the silencing of the pagan oracles, he nevertheless includes three elegiac stanzas (19–21) in which he imagines the nymphs mourning for the departing Greek and Roman gods. Rather than involving a full-scale rejection of classical forms and themes – after all, classical culture and literature were central to Milton's intellectual upbringing – his poems tend to involve revisionary transformations of them, infusing these earlier forms with new prophetic Christian meaning.

For all its virtuosity and emotional power, *Lycidas* is a poem which concludes by anticipating still greater, more ambitious projects. Virgil himself had established the progression in his career by beginning with pastoral (the *Eclogues*), and then moving from georgic to epic poetry. Like Virgil and Spenser before him (the latter poet moving from *The Shepheardes Calender* to *The Faerie Queene*), the new, yet obscure poet or "uncouth Swain" (186) of this poem has distinguished himself in his early career by writing in pastoral, regarded as the lowest of literary forms in the Renaissance; and like them, Milton, already self-consciously fashioning his career in the early prophetic poems, will go on to write the most ambitious of all forms, the epic. "Sunk low" (172), like Lycidas, this young, learned poet hopes, in his own way, to mount high. "Tomorrow to fresh Woods, and Pastures new" (193): using the language of pastoral, the ending of Milton's *Lycidas* looks forward to a new beginning, new genres, and future actions. (And yet rather than simply abandoning pastoral, *Paradise Lost*, we shall see, incorporates it in its vision of Eden.) But not until some twenty years later would Milton fully invest his great literary talents in his most ambitious poem.

3 Writing in the English Revolution and the Restoration

Until the late 1650s, Milton postponed the composition of his great poem and instead invested his literary talents in the tireless composition of revolutionary tracts and polemics, while also working (beginning in March 1649) as Oliver Cromwell's Latin Secretary. In order to understand *Paradise Lost* in relation to Milton's age and career, we need to remember that Milton spent almost twenty years (between 1641 and 1660) writing controversial prose works passionately defending ecclesiastical, domestic, and civil liberty, and attacking forms of ecclesiastical and political tyranny and idolatry. The Civil War and Interregnum years were a period of great religious and political upheaval in England – "tumultuous times" Milton called them (YP 1:807) – in which his contemporaries witnessed the abolition of episcopacy, kingship, and the House of Lords, as well as the execution of King Charles I and the establishment of the Commonwealth. In his antiprelatical tracts of the early 1640s, Milton himself vigorously opposed forms of episcopal power and church hierarchy; and in his antimonarchical, pro-republican tracts of 1649, as well as in his *Defenses of the English People* (1651, 1654), he attacked the symbolic representations of Stuart absolutism and power, along with the equivocal behavior of the Presbyterians who, by refusing to condemn Charles I, had betrayed the more radical Puritans committed to revolution. Milton's hatred of arbitrary rule in his polemical writings partly accounts for his condemnation of all earthly tyrannies in the prophetic books concluding *Paradise Lost*. Throughout his career, Milton continued to believe what he so bluntly stated in his *Tenure of Kings and Magistrates* (1649): "No man who knows ought, can be so stupid to deny that all men naturally were borne free" (YP 3:198). Always the iconoclast, he energetically smashed the lifeless idols of tradition and custom whenever they hindered the dynamic and ongoing process of ecclesiastical, domestic, and social reform. In his late pre-Restoration tracts (1659–60), he fearlessly urged his countrymen to resist the restoration of Stuart monarchy (which he compared to "chusing ... a captain back for *Egypt*," YP 7:463), while defending Christian liberty and condemning the forcing of the individual conscience in spiritual matters by outward authority. Like other radicals of his age – for example the Leveller writer William Walwyn or the Quakers – Milton defended the liberty of conscience. As a polemicist during the Civil War years and Interregnum, then, Milton became increasingly suspicious of institutional and centralized forms of secular power and external authority, preferring instead, as he does at the end of *Paradise Lost*, the authority found in the Bible, "those written Records pure" (12.513).

Milton's long career as revolutionary prose writer was itself important in the evolution of his literary vocation and contributed to the shaping of *Paradise Lost* in its prophetic themes and art. Indeed, Milton often channelled his creative energies into his prose, and the occasions provided by his controversial works enabled him to define what were to become central epistemological and vocational concerns of his poem. His prophetic stance, for example, is no less pronounced in the prose than in his epic: thus in *The Reason of Church-Government*, Milton compares himself in his divine inspiration to "those ancient profets" Jeremiah, Isaiah, and John of Revelation; as a zealous prophet of his age urging social and ecclesiastical reform, he too may have to utter odious truths in "sharp, but saving words," for "when God commands to take the trumpet and blow a dolorous or a jarring blast, it lies not in mans will what he shall say, or what he shall conceal" (YP 1:802–4). This would become the stance of the just men in the final books of *Paradise Lost*. Moreover, even while attacking the Anglican clergy with apocalyptic vehemence, Milton could make his rich and flamboyant prose "soare a while as the Poets use," as when he colourfully imagines the warrior "Zeale" in his fiery chariot punishing "Scarlet Prelats" under his flaming wheels (*An Apology for Smectymnuus*, YP 1:900).

One of the most pertinent prose texts for approaching *Paradise Lost* is *Areopagitica* (November 1644), Milton's famous attack on censorship. A work in which Milton employs densely figurative prose to explore the ethical issues of confrontation, trial, and temptation, *Areopagitica* engages themes central to *Paradise Lost*, where Milton dramatizes issues of human choice and free will. Written in opposition to Parliament's Licensing Order of 1643, *Areopagitica* (itself addressed to Parliament, especially its more tolerant members) argues that certain forms of censorship will only hinder the ongoing process of reformation and social change. This process, Milton believes, is stimulated by the Revolution's ferment of new radical political and spiritual ideas, by the proliferation of religious sects, and by the outpouring of controversial writing itself which challenges and disrupts tyrannical custom, mindless conformity and old orthodoxies. Milton represents Truth as a dynamic force: she is like a "streaming fountain" flowing "in a perpetuall progression," so that her waters do not "sick'n into a muddy pool of conformity

and tradition" (YP 2:543). By the end *Areopagitica* envisions the
rejuvenation of both the chosen nation Britannia ("a noble and
puissant Nation") and her visionary writer – John Milton himself –
while articulating passionately some of Milton's central social ideals, including the liberty of debate and combative discussion which
creates an atmosphere of "knowledge in the making" (YP 2:554).
Thus, virtue for Milton cannot simply be taken for granted, but must
be continually tested and, in effect, given real meaning through a
vigorous process of trial in which Truth grapples with Falsehood.
Rejecting the notion of "a blank vertue" with "an excrementall [i.e.
external] whitenesse," Milton asserts that "that which purifies us is
triall, and triall is by what is contrary" (YP 2:515–16), including
trial which involves active engagement with evil and inner struggle
with temptation. Milton's tract everywhere valorizes energetic conflict and confrontation, much as *Paradise Lost* will later do: like Eve,
as she responds to Adam in their critical pre-temptation discussion
in Book 9, Milton argues passionately against "a fugitive and clois-
ter'd vertue, unexercis'd & unbreath'd, that never sallies out and
sees her adversary" (YP 2:515).

In *Areopagitica*, Milton recognizes our constant need to engage
heroically with a world of evil and moral ambiguity "in the midd'st
whereof God hath plac't us unavoidably" (YP 2:526). Even Milton's
prelapsarian Eden, we shall see later, is a dynamic place where Adam
and Eve, confronted with numerous domestic and ethical challenges
and trials, do not lead a languorous existence but continually and
actively exercise their reason and freedom of choice. Some of *Paradise
Lost's* central themes are already imbedded in this rich passage from
Milton's pamphlet:

> many there be that complain of divin Providence for suffering *Adam* to
> transgresse, foolish tongues! when God gave him reason, he gave him
> freedom to choose, for reason is but choosing; he had bin else a meer
> artificiall *Adam*, such an *Adam* as he is in the motions. We our selves
> esteem not of that obedience, or love, or gift, which is of force: God
> therefore left him free, set before him a provoking object, ever almost
> in his eyes; herein consisted his merit, herein the right of his reward,
> the praise of his abstinence. Wherefore did he creat passions within us,
> pleasures round about us, but that these rightly temper'd are the very
> ingredients of vertu?   (YP 2:527)

Milton places great emphasis here, as he does in his poem, on the freedom and responsibility of human agents to choose; in this sense, his epistemology of freedom differs greatly from the severe Calvinist position which stresses that human reason and will are completely inadequate and depraved. Without free will, Adam would have been nothing more than a puppet – "a meer artificiall *Adam*" – with no will or mind of his own; the theatrical metaphor underscores the hollowness of such an Adam, an Adam who is no more than a mask like the player-king Charles I whom Milton attacked five years later. Milton's *Areopagitica* stresses the need to see and know "a provoking object" and yet abstain from it, as Spenser's Guyon does in the Cave of Mammon and the sensuous Bower of Earthly Bliss in Book 2 of *The Faerie Queene* (see YP 2:516). For without temptation and trial, without being tested in "the wars of Truth" (YP 2:562), and without the struggle of contrarieties, virtue itself would be as empty as an artificial Adam. Moreover, for all his emphasis on the importance of reason in the process of temptation and choice, Milton valorizes the passions within us, as well as the pleasures without – so long as they are tempered. And this, we shall see, is true in *Paradise Lost* where Milton presents, attractively and sympathetically, the complexities of human passion, while enabling his readers to enjoy – and almost taste – the pleasures of Eden.

The *Second Defense of the English People* (1654), another major prose work, also signaled a potential direction for his epic ambitions. Addressed to the European community at large, this Latin pamphlet celebrated the heroic achievements of a number of virtuous revolutionary leaders and Parliamentarians, including Cromwell himself, leader of the Protectorate, the regime that assumed power at the end of 1653. The *Second Defense* became an occasion for revolutionary mythmaking; there, Milton explicitly compared himself to an epic poet celebrating the heroic deeds of his glorious compatriots:

> just as the epic poet . . . undertakes to extol, not the whole life of the hero whom he proposes to celebrate in his verse, but usually one event of his life (the exploits of Achilles at Troy, let us say, or the return of Ulysses, or the arrival of Aeneas in Italy) and passes over the rest, so let it suffice me too . . . to have celebrated at least one heroic achievement of my countrymen.   (YP 4:685)

The *Second Defense* was a rhetorical performance which enabled Milton to channel his epic vision and literary talents directly into political prose writing. Indeed, the work reveals Milton's impulse to write an epic based not so much on legendary history as upon the major actors and exhilarating events of the Revolution, whose unfolding drama was so energetically engaging the writer's verbal and polemical skills during the 1640s and 1650s. Cromwell's deeds themselves, Milton claims, have outstripped "even the legends of our heroes" (YP 4:672). But in writing *Paradise Lost*, Milton, we have noted, chose not to restrict himself to immediate national concerns (however heroic), developing instead a more universal and international theme. By September 1658 Cromwell was dead and there would have been little to be gained, especially as the dark days of the Restoration approached, in composing a long poem honoring his epic-like deeds. As Milton the revolutionary writer observed in 1658, when he published a revised edition of his *First Defense*, "I am at this time hoping and planning still greater things" for the sake of "all Christian men" (YP 4:537) – quite possibly his large theological treatise, the *Christian Doctrine* (see section 5), or possibly *Paradise Lost* itself.

Our effort to situate *Paradise Lost* in relation to Milton's revolutionary writings, however, should not obscure the fact that his epic was written partly during the Restoration itself. That fact may prompt us to complicate our sometimes too neat sense of literary and historical periods. After all, the traditional way of approaching *Paradise Lost* as a landmark of world literature has been to see it as the most sublime product of Renaissance culture and especially as the last great epic of that age. But we need to remember as well its Restoration context: it was composed while Milton was still writing political tracts opposing the restoration of Stuart power and completed when the earthly monarchy had been restored and Milton's political ideals had been shattered. And with the Restoration came the return of the Church of England, the persecution of the Dissenting sects, and the resumption of strict censorship; the extraordinary outburst of millenarianism (the fervent belief in Christ's "shortly-expected" kingdom on earth, YP 1:616) that had made Milton's England a nation of prophets during the Civil War years and Interregnum was now largely checked. God's kingdom on earth had failed to come: the promised new paradise in England now seemed lost forever.

After the Restoration Milton regarded himself as something of a political exile within his own country: "One's *Patria* is wherever it is well with him" (YP 8:4), he observed to a correspondent in 1666. The famous English diarist, Samuel Pepys, concluded his account of that same year, the year before *Paradise Lost* was first published, with the following grim observation about the decadent Royalist court which Milton had defiantly opposed: "A sad, vicious, negligent Court, and all sober men there fearful of the ruin of the whole Kingdom this next year – from which, good God deliver us" (December 31). *Paradise Lost* at times keenly registers Milton's political isolation and disappointment with the Restoration, as well as the sense of political danger to the former radical writer and Puritan activist. Like Bunyan's *Pilgrim's Progress*, another major Puritan work of the Restoration years, *Paradise Lost* expresses its author's sense of social and spiritual adversity towards a culture and age whose secular values he despises and feels alienated from. Imprisoned for some weeks towards the end of 1660, Milton was lucky indeed to escape a rebel's execution: thus even while his poem's sacred theme clearly gives it a more universal and international appeal, the poem's immediate historical pressures can still poignantly be felt.

Paradise Lost, then, does not present the visionary writer in a land of prophets and among the Lord's people engaged in energetic social reform (as does *Areopagitica*). Rather, the lonely prophet who published and partly wrote his poem in the politically "cold / Climate" (9.44–5) of the Restoration finds himself

> fall'n on evil days,
> On evil days though fall'n, and evil tongues;
> In darkness, and with dangers compast round,
> And solitude.   (7.25–8)

Isolated in such a hostile world, like the defiant Abdiel among Satan's legions in Book 5, the poet remains "unchang'd" (7.24) in his fundamental principles and beliefs. Nevertheless, he fears "the barbarous dissonance / Of *Bacchus* and his Revellers, the Race / Of that wild Rout that tore the *Thracian* Bard" (7.32–4), lines recalling the alarming dismemberment or *sparagmos* of the legendary poet Orpheus (unprotected even by Calliope, his mother and muse of epic poetry) which Milton had lamented in *Lycidas*. The sacred poet of *Paradise Lost* is exposed to the dangers of a Satanic Restoration audience with their savagery and hostile tongues. Indeed, in 1660 he had referred to the "tigers of Bacchus" (YP 7:452–3) in the royalist court. Like the historical David, Milton himself hopes to be protected in his own time from the lying tongues of deadly enemies surrounding him (see Psalms 17:9 and 109:2). Such political references, moreover, underscore the precarious nature of the poet's solitary and daring enterprise. After all, *Paradise Lost*, Milton suggests in the invocation to Book 9, may have been completed and published in "an age too late" (44), a Restoration milieu unsympathetic to the imaginative boldness and originality of Milton's great Protestant epic.

Milton's note on the verse of *Paradise Lost*, added in the 1668 issue of the poem (and kept in subsequent editions), underscores his defensiveness and defiance as he writes in an insensitive age that may not adequately appreciate his daring literary achievements and ambitions. Clearly, many readers expected the poem, when it first appeared in 1667, to rhyme. Rhyme, after all, was in fashion among royalist writers in the Restoration, especially for the heroic poem: Sir William Davenant had used rhyme in his uncompleted heroic poem *Gondibert* (1651), and other poets of the age, including Edmund Waller, John Dryden, and Abraham Cowley, used it as well. According to Aubrey, Dryden even asked Milton's permission "to put his Paradise Lost into a Drama in Rhyme" and Milton, receiving him graciously, wittily told the poet "he would give him leave to tagge his Verses" (*Early Lives*, p. 7). But in *Paradise Lost*, where Milton chooses blank verse, he follows the examples of his great classical precursors and originals – "*Homer* in *Greek . . . Virgil* in *Latin*" – and consequently thinks rhyme is merely "the Invention of a barbarous Age, to set off wretched matter and lame Meter" (Hughes, p. 210). (Homer and Virgil had used unrhymed hexameters in their epic poems.) Milton scorns those "vulgar Readers" in this frivolous age who expect his epic poem to conform to such trifling literary conventions. He prefers a more discriminating or "fit audience" (7.31), cultured readers sharing his vision of political and religious reformation (like Marvell for example) who will appreciate the boldness of his prophetic enterprise and "vast Design" (to recall Marvell's phrase).

Choosing to resist the Restoration vogue for rhyme, Milton asserts that his practice "rather is to be esteem'd an example set, the first in *English*, of ancient liberty recover'd to Heroic Poem from the troublesome and modern bondage of Riming." Indeed, the political language here – the recovery of ancient liberty, the bondage of rhyme – suggests that Milton's decision to defy Restoration aesthetics and taste is by no means a purely literary matter.

4 Milton's blindness

When Milton tells us in the invocation to Book 7 that he exists "In darkness, and with dangers compast round, / And solitude" (27–8), he not only highlights his sense of isolation in the dangerous Restoration years, but also his blindness, with its poignant sense of enclosure and solitariness explored in the great invocations to *Paradise Lost* (see section 8). Milton had gone completely blind by February 1652, his sight having begun to fail as early as 1644: how was the ambitious poet, who envisioned himself as sacred and destined in his vocation, to respond to this traumatic event in his life and career? And what indeed was the effect of Milton's physical affliction (possibly caused by a cystic tumour or by chronic glaucoma) on his literary creativity and powers? As the bitterness and restlessness expressed in the first part of his sonnet "When I consider how my light is spent" (1652?) suggests, a blind and anxious Milton feared that he might turn out to be like the unprofitable servant of the Parable of Talents (Matthew 25:14–30) who, failing to yield his talent lodged "useless" within, is cast into outer darkness. Milton was the son of a money-lender and his reference to the Parable of Talents here reveals, as it does in sonnet 7, "How soon hath time," and *Ad Patrem*, that Milton hoped that the investment made in his poetic talents would yield a handsome return. Yet Milton's blindness in some sense also made him resolute and decisive as a poet, even if that meant further postponing his great poem: "They also serve who only stand and wait," he concludes his famous sonnet on blindness. Standing and waiting for "due time" when God will call is in fact precisely the theme Milton would explore in *Paradise Regained* (1671), where Jesus, tempted by Satan to act now when his years are "ripe," instead chooses to wait and stand. In contrast to the active angels who rush to serve "without rest" in "When I consider," the blind poet himself will wait for God's command, will reserve his enormous creative energy for the future, and will thereby make a strength out of his weakness.

Milton had long believed in "the mighty weaknes of the Gospel" to "throw down the weak mightiness of mans reasoning" (*Church-Government*, YP 1:827). Indeed, this notion of strength made perfect in weakness turned out to be crucial to his conception of the poet as *vates* – one who is a prophet and seer though blind – and contributed to the intense inwardness of his great poems. "My strength is made perfect in weakness," based on 2 Corinthians 12:9–10, became nothing less than the blind Milton's personal motto in the 1650s, one he would inscribe in autograph albums. The notion underlies Milton's *Second Defense* where, even as he writes as a public defender of the state, he includes a great deal of autobiographical material in defense of himself and his character. There, too, Milton attempts to make sense of his blindness: had he, after all, been punished by God with blindness for his savage polemics against King Charles I, as royalist propagandists had claimed? Having lost his eyes, as he writes in one of his sonnets, "overplied / In liberty's defense" ("To Mr. Cyriack Skinner"), Milton interprets his blindness in the *Second Defense* as no less than a divine gift, a distinctive mark of sacredness and artistic strength and an indication of spiritual, internal illumination:

> I shall be at once the weakest and the strongest, at the same time blind and most keen in vision. By this infirmity may I be perfected, by this completed . . . Divine law and divine favor have rendered us not only safe from the injuries of men, but almost sacred, nor do these shadows around us seem to have been created so much by the dullness of our eyes as by the shade of angels' wings. And divine favor not infrequently is wont to lighten these shadows again, once made, by an inner and far more enduring light.   (YP 4:590)

And so the righteous and unreproachable poet-polemicist may well be blind to the external world, but he is illuminated within and resembles David who is protected by the shadow of heavenly wings (see e.g. Psalms 17:8, 63:7). Milton wanted to believe, then, that blindness was by no means penal and that God would indeed exalt and protect his sacred poet, himself

> equall'd with them in renown,
> Blind *Thamyris* and blind *Maeonides*,
> And *Tiresias* and *Phineus* Prophets old.   (3.34–6)

As these lines from the invocation to Light in *Paradise Lost* suggest, the blind poet did not hesitate to compare his artistic and visionary powers to those of the mythic and blind seers and poets of the classical world, including Homer himself ("blind *Maeonides*"), depicted by ancient tradition as a blind singer. Moreover, in the midst of the politically hostile Restoration, the prophetic poet and revolutionary polemicist continued to assert, in his own personal way, the doctrine of the inner light associated especially with the more radical Puritan groups of his age (for example, the Quakers).

The Latin medical term for Milton's blindness was *gutta serena*, which means "drop serene" (3.25) or clear. His blind eyes, Milton responded in the *Second Defense* after being reviled by polemical enemies and called a Cyclops, "have as much the appearance of being uninjured, and are as clear and bright, without a cloud, as the eyes of men who see most keenly" (YP 4:583). Nevertheless, in the invocations to *Paradise Lost*, the blind poet continues to highlight his sense of darkness which requires internal illumination. With that gift he may undertake his visionary epic and assume his prophetic authority: "What in me is dark/Illumine" (1.22–3) Milton petitions the Holy Spirit at the outset of his poem, as he is about to begin his adventurous flight. On the one hand, this posture suggests Milton's fallenness ("all our woe" [1.3]), which he shares with all mankind; on the other hand, it suggests the blind Milton's enormous potential for inner vision, which he uniquely shares with the prophets of old.

We shall have further occasion to examine the issue of poetic creativity and authority in *Paradise Lost* (section 8). But for the moment we can highlight more concretely the way Milton dramatizes his blindness and the need for internal illumination by looking at the poignant catalogue of loss which concludes his invocation to Light in Book 3:

                                    Thus with the Year
          Seasons return, but not to me returns
          Day, or the sweet approach of Ev'n or Morn,
          Or sight of vernal bloom, or Summer's Rose,
          Or flocks, or herds, or human face divine;
          But cloud instead, and ever-during dark
          Surrounds me, from the cheerful ways of men
          Cut off, and for the Book of knowledge fair
          Presented with a Universal blanc
          Of Nature's works to me expung'd and ras'd,
          And wisdom at one entrance quite shut out.
          So much the rather thou Celestial Light
          Shine inward, and the mind through all her powers
          Irradiate, there plant eyes, all mist from thence
          Purge and disperse, that I may see and tell
          Of things invisible to mortal sight.   (40–55)

Milton's poetic invocations are unusual in developing such a deeply
personal and inward perspective, and this one is no exception, as
it focuses intensely on the meaning of his blindness, on his artistic creativity in relation to God's creative potency (symbolized by
the light), and on his need for inward vision. In the midst of the
Restoration's evil days, we noted, the daring poet and unrepentant
revolutionary felt himself encompassed by darkness and hostility;
here the solitary poet emphasizes the darkness surrounding him
as a consequence of his blindness, excluding him from temporal
and seasonal changes, from the pastoral world (the "flocks" and
"herds"), and from the "cheerful" world of human activities. Unable
to read the Book of Nature – "the Book of knowledge fair" – he simply perceives a "Universal blanc." But that "Universal blanc" or void
might also be regarded as a kind of *tabula rasa*; if blindness heightens the poet's tragic sense of exclusion and loss, it also underscores
his sense of creative potential – so long, that is, as God, who can
"fill/Infinitude" (7.168–9), responds to Milton's bold command to
"Shine" the "Celestial Light" inwardly. "There plant eyes": Milton's
metaphor conveys the sense of the potent beam of heavenly light
mating with seeds so as to generate new internal vision which will
illuminate his darkened mind. The poet whose light is spent has
endured the suffering and agony of blindness and now commands

God to repay him, to replace that loss of external sight with the gift of inner illumination. Milton's imperative stance here is indeed a daring one: it is the assertiveness of an ambitious blind bard who, willing here even to challenge God and demand his due, wishes to make a strength out of his weakness, so that his poetic and prophetic vision may far exceed that of "mortal sight."

5 Milton's theological heresies

Milton's vast theological treatise, *De Doctrina Christiana*, which systematically assembles thousands of scriptural passages, must have meant a great deal to the blind, solitary writer, for he considered it his "dearest and best possession" and his "greatest comfort" (YP 6:121). It is likely that Milton was composing the treatise by the late 1650s and that he was dictating revisions up until the time of his death. In recent years, questions have emerged about the nature of Milton's authorship, since the treatise was not discovered until 1823, but Milton's earliest biographers were well aware that he was working on a "Body of Divinity concerning some speculative points, differing . . . from that commonly received" (*Early Lives*, p. 31), and the connections between it and *Paradise Lost* are often remarkably close. The *Christian Doctrine* was an attempt to illuminate his "dark" mind with the texts and spirit of the Bible, which Milton, like other Puritans, valued above all other works: the Bible, he remarks in an early tract, is "the onely Book left us of *Divine* authority" (YP 1:625). Simultaneously as he was working on *Paradise Lost*, Milton was compiling his voluminous treatise on Biblical matters. Here we see Milton working out in a systematic way religious beliefs – some of them quite unorthodox – that would prove central to his poem. His heterodox theological ideas, we shall have occasion to see later, are crucial to *Paradise Lost* where he gives them poetic and dramatic expression. Before discussing the poem in detail, then, we should note several of Milton's important theological heresies, as well as some of their implications for his intellectual and imaginative development.

In keeping with the iconoclastic and independent-minded temperament characteristic of his other writings, the *Christian Doctrine* was also written with the hope that his work might, as its prefatory epistle says, help "wipe away those two repulsive afflictions, tyranny and superstition, from human life and the human mind" (YP 6:118) and thus challenge human traditions and idolatrous authorities so that "the citadel of reformed religion was adequately fortified against the Papists" (120). Like other Puritans of his age, Milton had deeply resented the liturgical innovations of Archbishop William Laud (d. 1645) who had subordinated the status of Scripture and individual conscience by emphasizing the Church of England's power and ceremonialism. With its clergy, sacraments, ornate vestments, ceremonies and rituals, and emphasis on the sanctity of the altar, the Church under Laud had asserted its splendor and authority in idolatrous ways that struck Puritans like Milton as nothing less than Popery. Like other Protestants, Milton believed that "God has revealed the way of eternal salvation only to the individual faith of each man" (YP 6:118); and since "God's word alone [is] the rule of faith" (YP 6:203), Milton's principal authority is not the state or church, but Scripture itself, for him a vital and dynamic spiritual force both in his age and within the upright heart of each Protestant individual.

As a radical Protestant, Milton recognizes that many of his theological views in the *Christian Doctrine* "are at odds with certain conventional opinions" and, as he did in *Areopagitica*, he valorizes "free discussion and inquiry" as he seeks "tirelessly after truth" (YP 6:120–1). His treatise reveals how he rethinks established theological doctrine. For one thing, it reveals Milton to be anti-Trinitarian in his theological beliefs, unlike the more conventional young prophetic poet of the Nativity Ode who had referred to the "Trinal Unity" (line 11) in heaven. Anti-Trinitarianism was itself widespread in England among radical Protestants during the 1640s and 1650s. In the *Christian Doctrine* Milton dismantles the orthodox Trinity so that the Son, though divine, is clearly subordinate to the Father and has an independent identity subject to change and lacking the Father's omniscience, omnipresence, and omnipotence. The Son was the first of all created things and thus his generation or begetting by God (with his own free will, Milton emphasizes) was not from eternity – as Augustine, for example, had argued – but "within the bounds of time" (YP 6:209), distinguishing him from the uncreated, immutable, and eternal Father (as in *PL* 3.372ff.). The sacred song of the angels in Book 3 of *Paradise Lost* calls attention to Milton's heresy by highlighting the creation of the Son and his subordination to the Father from whom he derives his power and strength:

> Thee next they sang of all Creation first,
> Begotten Son, Divine Similitude,
> In whose conspicuous count'nance, without cloud
> Made visible, th' Almighty Father shines,
> Whom else no Creature can behold; on thee
> Impresst th' effulgence of his Glory abides,
> Transfus'd on thee his ample Spirit rests.   (383–9)

Although the "Begotten Son" shares in the Father's substance (see *PL* 3.138–40), the Father and Son are not one in essence or co-essential, Milton believes, and consequently, the Father is greater than the Son "in all things" (YP 6:223). The Son's divine nature, then, is distinct from and inferior to the Father's. Since there was not a word in the Holy Scriptures in support of the mystery of the Trinity ("Reason rejects the idea, and scripture nowhere supports it," YP 6:239), Milton found himself diverging from the orthodox view by emphasizing filial subordinationism in treatise and poem. His independent-minded response to the Trinity is a good example of how Milton attempts "to puzzle out a religious creed for [himself] by [his] own exertions" (YP 6:118), and then give it imaginative expression.

Milton's theological exertions, moreover, revealed his heretical materialist assumptions: neither in his treatise nor in *Paradise Lost* does Milton follow the more orthodox notion that God created the universe *ex nihilo* (from nothing); instead, God created *ex deo* (i.e. from out of himself or his substance) and *ex materia* (from matter). Milton concludes that matter was essentially "a passive principle" and must have originated from a material God – principal "Author and end of all things" (*PL* 7.591) – at some point. Nor was original matter evil in Milton's view: "it was good, and it contained the seeds of all subsequent good. It was a substance, and could only have been derived from the source of all substance. It was in a confused and disordered state at first, but afterwards God made it ordered and beautiful" (YP 6:307–8). In *Paradise Lost*, Milton represents Chaos itself as primal matter in a warring state divorced from providential order and goodness (see e.g. 2.894ff.). Milton's philosophical materialism becomes rich poetic substance in the dynamic cosmos of *Paradise Lost* where, as we shall see later (in section 15), spirit and matter are altogether inseparable – "one first matter all" (5.472) as Raphael teaches Adam. The heretical Protestant poet consequently rejects traditional Christian dualisms in both treatise and poem, preferring instead a universe characterized by its materiality.

Of all of Milton's unorthodox theological beliefs, his radical Arminianism is perhaps the most significant one for understanding *Paradise Lost*. This refers to his passionate belief in human free will which distinguished him from more orthodox Calvinist Puritans of his day, as well as from such leading Reformation theologians as Luther, Calvin, Zwingli, among others. These Reformation theologians stressed that man's nature was so debased and enslaved by sin that it precluded his ability to achieve salvation through the use of his free will. Typical of the Reformation view of free will, especially in regard to religious matters, was the following uncompromising assertion made by Luther in 1525 in his famous debate with Erasmus over this issue: "with regard to God, and in all that bears on salvation or damnation, [man] has no 'free will,' but is a captive, prisoner and bondslave, either to the will of God, or to the will of Satan" (*De Servo Arbitrio* [*The Bondage of the Will*], trans. J. I. Packer and O. R. Johnston [1957], p. 107); indeed, to ascribe free will to man, thereby endowing him with divine powers, was nothing less than blasphemy according to Luther. We have seen that Milton's *Areopagitica* gives unusual emphasis to human freedom and the active responsibility that comes with it. But in *Areopagitica* the libertarian Milton was not quite yet Arminian in his theological convictions as he clearly is in the *Christian Doctrine* and in *Paradise Lost*. Milton had read the Dutch theologian, Jacobus Arminius (d. 1609), who had posited a more Pelagian challenge to Calvinism by stressing that individuals were free to accept or reject the divine grace needed for salvation – in contrast to Calvinism's intensely negative view of human agency and will. Adam himself recognizes the importance of the gift of free will when he tells Eve, just before she goes off on her own in Book 9, that "God left free the Will, for what obeys / Reason, is free" (351–2). Believing that we are not mere puppets when it comes to matters of salvation and not wholly dependent on God's irresistible grace, Milton was especially attracted to the notion that humans act freely, a theme central to the theological debate in Book 3 of *Paradise Lost* (see section 12), but not at all compatible with the stricter Calvinist theology dominating English Protestantism in the early seventeenth century. Milton thus found himself diverging from mainstream Calvinist and Puritan doctrine: he wanted to insist on the value of human free will, unlike Calvin who emphasized only God's immutable decrees and omnipotence, along with man's utter depravity, powerlessness, and "infected will" (as the Protestant poet Sir Philip Sidney called it).

Likewise, Milton found himself diverging from the predestinarian orthodoxy asserted by traditional Calvinist Puritans of his age – the fundamental notion that men are irrevocably predestined by God to salvation or perdition. Milton stressed God's foreknowledge in his *Christian Doctrine* and *Paradise Lost*, but firmly wished to deny that future events (though they might be in the mind of the foreknower) were predestined or happened by necessity ("Necessity and Chance / Approach not mee," says Milton's God [7.172–3]). In attempting to "justify the ways of God to men" in *Paradise Lost*, Milton was also attempting to differentiate his God from the Calvinist God of arbitrary power. The concept of freedom, with its implications of human responsibility, means that Adam and Eve cannot "justly accuse" God

> As if Predestination over-rul'd
> Thir will, dispos'd by absolute Decree
> Or high foreknowledge; they themselves decreed
> Thir own revolt, not I: if I foreknew,
> Foreknowledge had no influence on their fault,
> Which had no less prov'd certain unforeknown.

So Milton's God defensively observes in the heavenly colloquy of *Paradise Lost* (3.112–19), a section of the poem many readers find theologically and emotionally unsettling. The Arminian message here is clear: God does indeed foresee events, but humankind may choose freely to stand or fall (as can angels, as we shall see later); when it comes to temptation, the choice is always ours since, as Milton observes in the *Christian Doctrine*, "there can be no absolute divine decree about the action of free agents" (YP 6:164) and thus we must banish "all idea of necessity" (161). And since it was not divinely determined, the Fall was by no means inevitable. Still, the harshness of God's words, particularly the emphasis in these lines on mankind's "fault" (cf. 3.96), brings out a tension at the very heart of Milton's theology, and one powerfully dramatized in his poem (as we shall see in section 12): this is a Protestant poet who attempts imaginatively to highlight the freedom of human agency, though without ever abandoning a belief in God's omnipotence.

Chapter 2

Interpreting *Paradise Lost*

6 "Say first what cause": *Paradise Lost* and beginnings

After its opening invocation, *Paradise Lost* launches into its first bold question, which begins the vast narrative of Milton's poem:

> Say first, for Heav'n hides nothing from thy view
> Nor the deep Tract of Hell, say first what cause
> Mov'd our Grand Parents in that happy State,
> Favor'd of Heav'n so highly, to fall off
> From thir Creator, and transgress his Will
> For one restraint, Lords of the World besides? (1.27–32)

This passage, which announces some of the key themes of Milton's sacred poem – the transgression of our original parents, their fall from their happy state, the omniscience of Milton's God – concerns itself with "first" things, including "Man's First Disobedience" (1.1). The word "first" significantly occurs six times in the poem's opening thirty-three lines. *Paradise Lost* thus immediately announces itself as a sacred poem about origins and beginnings – a poem that bases its great story on the Bible, the first of all texts for Protestants, and specifically on Genesis (especially chapters 1–3), itself the book of origins and beginnings. Indeed, Milton's first invocation explicitly echoes the first words of Genesis – "In the Beginning . . ." (1.9). And yet this is a poem about origins that will go beyond its Biblical source to inquire about causes, an impulse that even our original father will manifest in Milton's story (see 7.90ff.). In its attempt to fulfill its theodicy, to "assert Eternal Providence, / And justify the ways of God to men" (1.26–7), *Paradise Lost* also boldly attempts to explain the causes and origins of evil. To do this, Milton engages in the imaginative enterprise of Christian mythmaking: he has composed a long, ambitious visionary poem that not only narrates the story of the tragic fall of mankind, but explains how it first came about.

The Genesis story, after all, does not ask "what cause" brought about the fall of first man and woman. Its terse and sometimes enigmatic details do not supply, as Milton's immense epic does, an elaborate narrative and drama exploring the motives leading to the Fall, nor the complex psychology, emotions, and unusual intimacy of Adam and Eve. Nor does the Biblical text explain the presence and motives of the subtle serpent in Eden; nor how he happens to possess the power of speech. In Genesis, Eve seems to be alone when the serpent confronts her (the Bible is somewhat ambiguous here), and there is no explanation given for why he is enticing her and putting her obedience to the test. Yet in Book 9 of *Paradise Lost*, Milton gives his readers a detailed and brilliant account of the stages of the temptation and Fall (based on Genesis 3). And he creates, in the poem's opening books, the first two of which he sets in Hell, a powerful myth of anterior evil that explains the reasons for the infernal serpent's presence in Eden, as well as his hateful and vengeful motives for seducing our primal mother and father "to that foul revolt" (1.33). Milton's poem thus invents a mythic explanation: Satan, we find out, is an emissary from Hell and the Titanic adversary of God attempting to destroy the world and conquer God's new creation, the race of mankind. Quite unlike Genesis, then, Milton's sacred epic is deeply concerned with causes and origins and shows its readers how "Man falls deceiv'd / By th' other first" (3.130–1).

And so Milton's *Paradise Lost* asserts its own originality from its very beginning. It does so not only as an ambitious prophetic poem that thoroughly transforms the epic tradition, as we shall see in the next section, but also as a poem whose vast, etiological narrative about human loss and restoration takes his readers well beyond his scriptural source. *Paradise Lost* imaginatively attempts to soar above the "*Aonian Mount*" (1.15) – Mount Helicon, the sacred haunt of the classical Muses – and it attempts to probe deeper into the mystery of origins than the Holy Bible itself, the Protestant poet's principal authority. Part of this poem's own originality and boldness is due to its imaginative attempt to revise its Biblical and classical models.

And in the case of the classical and Renaissance epic, *Paradise Lost* revises the great genre upon which it is based in strikingly new ways.

7 "To raise / That Name": *Paradise Lost* and epic ambition

In writing his sublime poem, Milton was attempting to compose and revise what was by far the most ambitious, expansive, and encyclopedic of all literary genres – the epic. Indeed, Renaissance poets and critics regarded the epic or "the Heroical" as the highest form of literature – "the best and most accomplished kind of poetry," in the words of Sir Philip Sidney. Throughout *Paradise Lost* Milton is intensely self-conscious of himself writing in this ambitious and comprehensive form and attempting to do something entirely new with it. His was a highly challenging and risky undertaking. Already by the age of Virgil (70–19BC), the epic as a genre had been well-established. The following features, among others, were formulated long before by Homer: the beginning *in medias res* (in "the midst of things," as Milton's Argument to Book 1 says), the invocation of a muse, the emphasis on aristocratic and martial themes, the legendary heroes and exploits, the epic journey, the use of long similes and epic catalogues, and the intermixing of the deeds of gods and men. So too Milton, writing in a much later age, knows his epic models, as well as the rules and high standards and grand scale of this most demanding genre.

We have already noted in section 1 that Milton diverges from previous classical and Renaissance models – Virgil, Spenser, the sixteenth-century Portuguese poet Camoens, and others – by choosing not to write an epic on a more traditional national and imperialistic theme, and instead giving his long narrative poem more universal subject matter and much greater interior emphasis. In many ways, *Paradise Lost*, for all its apparent classical and epic features, is remarkably critical of pagan values whose heroic and martial codes it continually reevaluates. After all, the character in *Paradise Lost* who most nearly embodies the old-style martial virtues and heroic ideology of the epic tradition – as he manifests the rage of Achilles, as well as the skill and cunning of Odysseus – is Satan in his unwavering pursuit of personal glory and imperial ambitions (see especially sections 10 and 16). What is important to see about *Paradise Lost* is the way the great visionary poem positions itself within the epic tradition, which it boldly transforms in order to suit the intensely inward and Protestant emphases of Milton's Biblical inspiration, themes, and imagination.

Paradise Lost is continually ranging itself against previous epics, particularly in its invocations. The poem's remarkable opening lines immediately establish this relation and rivalry:

> Of Man's First Disobedience, and the Fruit
> Of that Forbidden Tree, whose mortal taste
> Brought Death into the World, and all our woe,
> With loss of *Eden*, till one greater Man
> Restore us, and regain the blissful Seat,
> Sing Heav'nly Muse . . .

Like other epic poets, Milton begins with an invocation that underscores his sense of literary performance in the ambitious tradition in which he boldly situates his sacred poem. Like the *Odyssey* or the *Aeneid*, Milton's long poem will also be about "man" (Adam rather than the wandering Odysseus and the fate-driven Aeneas) and his actions, though Milton's epic, unlike Virgil's, is neither named after nor concentrates upon a single hero. Like the *Iliad*, Milton's poem will also be about "Death," which is not only a subject or abstraction in *Paradise Lost* but an allegorical character and perverse offspring of Satan. Nothing, however, is said in these lines (nor in the rest of the invocation) about that most prominent of epic subjects – warfare, that major subject of the *Iliad* and the *Aeneid*, as well as many Renaissance epics. Warfare is indeed important in Milton's poem, as the cataclysmic war in Heaven (where Satan, Michael, and the Son all act as warriors) makes amply clear, but its older-style heroic values associated with martial epic are placed under close scrutiny and thoroughly challenged, and so Milton does not begin his poem as, say, the *Aeneid* does – *Arma virumque cano* ("I sing of arms and the man") – by focusing on "arms."

Milton's focus at the beginning of his poem is startlingly new: he is writing an epic about a great sacred theme. The sweep of his poem will move typologically from the Old Testament to the

New, from the first Adam to the second (Christ, that "one greater Man," rather than Virgil's Augustus prefigured by Aeneas), as the negative history of loss (of Paradise rather than Troy) is significantly broken in the middle of line 4 of the invocation by the future history of restoration. Milton thus immediately announces his poem as a Christian or Biblical epic and, even more specifically, as a prophetic Protestant epic, as his visionary invocation then goes on to sing of Moses, that inspired prophet ("That Shepherd, who first taught the chosen Seed") and author of the Pentateuch. Sweeping in its historical time scheme – "coeval with time itself," as Milton put it in one of his Prolusions (YP 1:297) – this sublime Protestant epic will move, like the Bible itself, from the Creation to the end of time.

The relation of Milton's ambitious prophetic poem to its classical precursors is made even more explicit in the invocation's subsequent lines describing his

> advent'rous Song,
> That with no middle flight intends to soar
> Above th' *Aonian* Mount, while it pursues
> Things unattempted yet in Prose or Rhyme.

The image of flight here (we think of Satan's own adventurous flight in the poem, as well as the presumptuous behavior of the "advent'rous *Eve*," 9.921) registers the extraordinary ambition of the inspired Protestant poet in this risk-taking enterprise: with the help and inspiration of his Heavenly Muse, he will soar above the classical Mount Helicon ("th' *Aonian* Mount"), sacred to the Muses, all the way to the realm of God and "the Heav'n of Heav'ns" (7.13). The sacred subject matter of his inspired poem, as he asserts in Book 9, is "Not less but more Heroic" (14) than that of his classical precursors whose heroic values his poem continually challenges, subverts, and transcends. Indeed, not only will Milton soar higher than any classical epic poet, but higher than any Christian poet as well. "Things unattempted yet in Prose or Rhyme" conveys Milton's ambitious claim to raise the name of epic to a new height (cf. 9.43–4), as he ironically echoes a similar claim to novelty made by Ariosto in 1516 at the beginning of his great romance epic, *Orlando Furioso* ("Cosa non detta in prosa mai, ne in rima," Canto 1.2). Of course, quite unlike Ariosto, whose poem combines chivalric and epic materials, this visionary poet has no interest in singing "Of Dames, of knights, of arms, of love's delight, / Of courtesies" (*Orlando* I.1, trans. Sir John Harrington), as his sacred poem ranges beyond his epic precursors and even beyond the Mosaic text itself (as we saw in section 6).

Addressing the Holy Spirit, Milton defines further the distinctly Protestant nature of his poem, so strikingly different from his precursors: the Spirit "dost prefer / Before all Temples th'upright heart and pure" (17–18). The drama of this poem's ambitious action is not only the entire cosmos including Heaven and Hell (as Marvell immediately appreciated in his verse commentary on *Paradise Lost*), but indeed the mind and heart of the Protestant individual. God does "not dwell in these temples which men had commanded and set up, but in people's hearts": thus Milton's contemporary George Fox the Quaker observes in his famous *Journal* (ed. J. Nickalls [1952], p. 8). So, too, in terms of spiritual focus, Milton's great Puritan epic takes a radical turn inward, not only by boldly rejecting the martial and imperial values of its pagan and Renaissance epic models, but by rejecting all external religious authorities as well. In this way, Milton's poem begins by striking a note of epic ambition, while announcing its aim to revise radically the tradition and swerve away from its older heroic values of outward trials and warfare, as it transforms the epic into a much more interior mode of spiritual trial and visionary poetry. As much as any other passage in *Paradise Lost*, this first invocation self-consciously identifies Milton's revisionary epic as truly a "landmark of world literature."

Elsewhere, for example in the invocation to Book 9, Milton continues to define the peculiar nature of his inspired epic enterprise, and to call attention to his competition with ancient epics. There, where Milton turns to his tragic theme, he sadly acknowledges the judgement and anger of heaven at mankind's disobedience and "distaste" which his narrative now will have to relate:

> Sad task, yet argument
> Not less but more Heroic than the wrath
> Of stern *Achilles* on his Foe pursu'd
> Thrice Fugitive about *Troy* Wall; or rage
> Of *Turnus* for *Lavinia* disespous'd,
> Or *Neptune's* ire or *Juno's*, that so long
> Perplex'd the *Greek* and *Cytherea's* Son.   (9.13–19)

Milton here evokes the wrath of heroes and gods in classical epic, as well as the suffering of epic heroes, in order to contrast his epic poem with its precursors. Anger or wrath is indeed one of the great subjects of epic poetry and the very first theme announced in the *Iliad* ("Anger be now your song, immortal one . . ."). But Milton will write of a divine anger which supersedes the anger of epic heroes (the wrathful and vengeful Achilles pursuing and slaying Hector, the furious wrath of Turnus in the final books of the *Aeneid*) and which, indeed, supersedes the anger of the gods of classical epic (the capricious anger and judgement of Poseidon ["Neptune"] towards Odysseus, the destructive wrath and bitterness of Juno towards Aeneas and the Trojans). Anger, after all, as a theme is no less central to Milton's poem than to its classical counterparts: both Satan and God manifest it, though Satan's is closer to the classical anger of Achilles or even to the fury of the hateful and obsessive Juno, while God's *odium* (his "just avenging ire" [7.184]) is more Biblical in character. Moreover, Christian tragedy, Milton's passage suggests, is more exact and less arbitrary in its justice than its classical models: though it may involve suffering (the "woe" which all humankind shares, not just epic heroes), as well as holy wrath, it does not perplex and bewilder, and its justice and God are not capricious like the behavior and justice of pagan gods. Milton's sacred narrative, then, will thoroughly transcend its pagan models in its account of justice and divine judgement.

Milton's invocation does not only range his poem against classical epic models; it also provides a more extended critical commentary on the relation of his "Heroic Song" to romantic and chivalric epic:

Not sedulous by Nature to indite
Wars, hitherto the only Argument
Heroic deem'd, chief maistry to dissect
With long and tedious havoc fabl'd Knights,
In Battles feign'd; the better fortitude
Of Patience and Heroic Martyrdom
Unsung; or to describe Races and Games,
Or tilting Furniture, emblazon'd Shields,
Impreses quaint, Caparisons and Steeds;
Bases and tinsel Trappings, gorgeous Knights
At Joust and Tournament . . .   (9.27ff.)

When Milton tells us that his long poem differs in crucial ways from that other long poem highly popular in the Renaissance – the romantic epic – he has in mind such texts as Sidney's *Arcadia* and Spenser's *Faerie Queene* ("tinsel Trappings," for instance, recalls the appearance of the beautiful Florimell's steed at 3.1.15), as well as continental chivalric romances by Boiardo, Tasso, and Ariosto. Milton suggests the superiority of his sacred subject matter to the fabulous and legendary subjects of chivalric poetry, even as his lines reveal his attraction to the language of romance, which he elaborates here. But there is yet another point to Milton's criticism: the digressive romance epic, he finds, is "long and tedious" and too much concerned with surface details, whereas the poetry of *Paradise Lost* is extraordinarily concentrated without sacrificing rich sensuousness. And, indeed, the full meaning of Milton's interior Protestant poem does seem to be contained within and to exfoliate from certain richly textured passages – its dense invocations, to cite only the most obvious examples.

There are many points at which *Paradise Lost* reminds us that its sacred themes and Biblical authority rival and supersede its epic precursors and their mythology. One telling passage from Book 1, the famous description of Mulciber, Pandemonium's architect, may serve to illustrate how Milton's Protestant poem carefully distances itself from pagan fable, the stuff of classical epic:

> Nor was his name unheard or unador'd
> In ancient *Greece*; and in *Ausonian* land
> Men call'd him *Mulciber*; and how he fell
> From Heav'n, they fabl'd, thrown by angry *Jove*
> Sheer o'er the Crystal Battlements: from Morn
> To Noon he fell, from Noon to dewy Eve,
> A Summer's day; and with the setting Sun
> Dropt from the Zenith like a falling Star,
> On *Lemnos* th' *Aegaean* Isle: thus they relate,
> Erring.   (1.738–47)

This passage richly evokes the mythic world and conflicts of classical epic (including the wrathful deity), while specifically alluding to the fall of Hephaestus recounted in *The Iliad* (Book 1). In *Paradise Lost*, the values and deeds of the fallen angels are often measured in terms of the myths and values of pagan epic. Here the poet emphasizes the fictional nature of Mulciber's great fall with carefully-placed phrases like "they fabl'd" and "thus they relate, / Erring." Indeed, the emphasis of that key word "Erring" explodes the mythology of classical epic, reminding Milton's readers that it is less than truthful, a distortion of that sacred and prior history of the Fall. In this way Milton distinguishes the sacred authority of his Protestant poem from classical fable – even as he is attracted by it. Milton's ambitious sacred epic may owe much to its classical sources and predecessors, but it also soars well beyond them: as this passage of mythic falling suggests, Hell is about as remote from Earth or Heaven (for both places, unlike Hell, experience "dewy Eve") as the erring fable of ancient epic is from the sacred truths of *Paradise Lost*. And so as Milton's highly original Protestant poem raises the name of epic to newer visionary heights, while giving that literary tradition a much greater interiority, it also distances itself critically from the authority of classical lore, myth, and literature.

8 The voice of the poet

In Milton's Protestant epic, the narrator's presence, inner life, and emotional responses are often highlighted and explored in the great invocations, as well as in many other passages throughout the poem. Indeed, the poet's voice in *Paradise Lost* is one of the most distinctive and individualistic in English literature. Michael Silk's apt description of "the narrator's impersonal stance" in Homer's *Iliad* (*Homer: The Iliad*, p. 99) would hardly apply to Milton's Puritan epic and its visionary poet. Seventeenth-century England, after all, was a great age of diaries, memoirs, and Puritan autobiographies of various kinds (one thinks of famous ones by John Bunyan, George Fox, Richard Baxter, among others). Milton's invocations, which explore his poetic authority, his literary ambition and vocation, and his creative relation to God's power, owe their inwardness in part to an age that produced significant spiritual writings of individuality, self-revelation, and radical self-analysis. But the strong presence and frequent intrusions of the poet in *Paradise Lost*, we shall also see, operate in other important ways as well: throughout the vast narrative, his magisterial and critical voice guides and shapes the reader's responses to the characters, events, and implications of his great poem. Moreover, the poet often responds himself with considerable emotion, at times unable to disengage his personal feelings from the momentous story he is narrating.

In the invocations to Books 1, 3, 7, and 9, Milton's personal voice emerges and assumes dramatic force. (We need not insist, as commentators sometimes do, on a firm distinction between the narrator and the historical figure John Milton.) Milton presents himself as inspired and prophetic, and one is struck immediately, as Andrew Marvell was upon reading Milton's poem, by the sheer daring of his prophetic enterprise, which transcends all pagan, Renaissance, and Old Testament precursors. Milton establishes his unusual poetic authority and line of vision by aligning himself at the beginning with the prophetic Moses, author of the Pentateuch ("That Shepherd, who first taught the chosen Seed," 1.8), as well as with Christ in his prophetic mission ("the Oracle of God," 1.12), as he invokes the Heavenly Muse's aid to his "advent'rous Song" (1.13).

But Milton also presents himself in the invocations as fallen like his readers and in need of restoration like the rest of humankind. His great poem, after all, will sing of "all *our* woe" (emphasis added) as he writes in the opening invocation, and that key phrase – "our woe" – resonates at other points (e.g. 2.872, 3.633, 9.645), underscoring the poet's own elegiac sense of loss and reminding us, his fallen audience, of his own participation in "this frail World" (2.1030). Further acknowledging his inner darkness – both his blindness and fallenness – Milton prays in the opening invocation to the Holy Spirit that he may be illuminated inwardly: "What in me is dark / Illumine, what is low raise and support" (1.22–3). So, too, in the proem to Book 7 the solitary poet sings "with mortal voice," again suggesting his own frailty despite his exceptional visionary powers. "May I express thee unblam'd?" (3.3) he asks in his invocation to Light, where he probes the divine origins and power of his own poetic creativity: the rhetorical question likewise conveys a sense of human discourse as fallible, as well as the poignant sense of *Paradise Lost* as a fallen poem. The invocations thus portray the blind poet from a dual perspective: as fallible and fallen like all men and yet as visionary and prophetic – as actively seeking inner illumination and the *visio dei* so that he may "see and tell / of things invisible to mortal sight"

(3.54–5) and (in the words of Satan) "Ascend to Heav'n . . . and see / What life the Gods live there" (5.80–1).

The poet, moreover, characterizes his relation to his creative process and Muse in paradoxical terms: when he invokes his "Celestial Patroness" in Book 9, he observes that she "dictates to me slumb'ring, or inspires / Easy my unpremeditated Verse" (23–4). On the one hand, Milton is an amanuensis taking down, during the Muse's nightly visitations, God's Word and the vast poem she dictates to him; on the other hand, he is the inspired Protestant poet, actively and spontaneously composing *Paradise Lost*. But without the aid, protection, and inspiration of his Heavenly Muse, the poet fears his ability to raise the name of epic to unprecedented heights in an age too late (like Restoration England) or in a cold climate which congeals his literary spirits – especially "*if* all be mine, / Not Hers who brings it nightly to my Ear" (9.46–7; emphasis added). Milton here anxiously reminds us of Satan close "at the ear of *Eve*" (4.800ff.) during the night: without a Heavenly Muse to intervene in his creative process, Milton suggests, his poem might indeed resemble a Satanic dream. The reference to the violent dismemberment of the mythic poet Orpheus in the invocation to Book 7 (lines 33–8) – "nor could the Muse defend / Her Son" – especially underscores Milton's anguished sense that even the sacred poet may find himself vulnerable to hostile (Restoration) readers, unprotected by his Muse. The invocations thus vacillate between expressing Milton's exhilarated sense of inspired authority and revealing his more troubling sense of uncertainty about his perilous enterprise.

A number of the poem's perceptive readers (e.g. Riggs, Kerrigan) have aptly noted that parallels suggested between the poet and Satan underscore the ambition and dangers of Milton's adventurous undertaking: both the poet and Satan engage in bold "flight" through darkness and escape "the *Stygian* Pool" (as the poet does at 3.14; cf. 1.239–40); both are solitary and self-enclosed (Milton by his blindness); both are "dark" and "low" at the beginning of the poem; both engage in forms of presumptuous seeing; and both of course are in their own ways creators and authors – Satan of "all ill" (2.381) and "dark designs" (1.213). Such parallels indeed suggest the poet's anxieties about his risky poetic undertaking – his solitary epic quest and ambition. Might not his vast design, which so unabashedly transgresses literary and even sacred boundaries to create a work "unattempted yet in Prose or Rhyme," be Satanic or even "impious" (1.43) in some way? In a poem that often recommends the virtues of being "lowly wise" (8.173) and submissive – trouble "not thy thoughts with matters hid" (167) Raphael tells Adam – the poet himself is aware that he appears to be one of its most presumptuous aspirers. The poem thus associates disturbing implications with Milton's adventurous composition, even if it eventually dispels them. After all, the inspired Milton, unlike the defiant Satan who insists that he is self-begotten and "Alone, and without guide" (2.975), never turns away from his divine creator, towards whom Satan shows such intense hatred. Ultimately the poem, for all its daring ambition and great risks, aligns Milton's poetic art and matter with the creative agency of the Son and the Father, "Author of all being" (3.374; 3.412–15). Unlike Satan, the visionary poet never claims that he and his powers are "self-begot."

Looking at two passages from the invocations, we can see further how the blind prophetic poet expresses his inwardness and presents his ambitious visionary enterprise; the first is from the second part of the invocation to Light, just after Milton has been addressing the "holy Light," a trope for the Deity and the divine origin of Milton's creative powers:

> Thee I revisit now with bolder wing,
> Escap't the *Stygian* Pool, though long detain'd
> In that obscure sojourn, while in my flight
> Through utter and through middle darkness borne
> With other notes than to th' *Orphean* Lyre
> I sung of *Chaos* and *Eternal Night*,
> Taught by the heav'nly Muse to venture down
> The dark descent, and up to reascend,
> Though hard and rare.   (3.13–21)

The parallel between the bold, solitary flights of Milton and Satan is reinforced by the fact that we have just been watching, at the end of Book 2, Satan voyage through Chaos on his "obscure sojourn" towards earth: both indeed are moving from darkness to light. The poet's own metaphorical flight through darkness, he suggests, has in fact been no less arduous and epic-like, no less daring and risky than Satan's: having descended to Hell, as Aeneas and the mythic Orpheus had done, he now reascends to the realm of light, in search of internal, spiritual illumination. Focusing our attention on his "hard" flight, the difficulty of his poetic task, the courageous Protestant poet himself becomes the heroic subject of his invocation. He refers not only to the darkness of Hell and Chaos, but to the darkness of his blindness, which reinforces his intense feelings of isolation and self-enclosure. But as he makes his "hard" journey to the realm of heavenly light, the poet anxiously hopes, in his desire for new and inward vision, not to be tantalized and punished by a judging God, much as Satan and the devils repeatedly find themselves throughout the poem: "thou / Revisit'st not these eyes, that roll in vain / To find thy piercing ray, and find no dawn" (3.22–4).

The motif of the poet's precarious, exhilarating flight recurs in the invocation to Book 7, where he addresses Urania ("the heavenly one"), Muse of astronomy and sacred poetry and the poem's "Celestial Patroness" (9.21):

> Up led by thee
> Into the Heav'n of Heav'ns I have presum'd,
> An Earthly Guest, and drawn Empyreal Air,
> Thy temp'ring; with like safety guided down
> Return me to my Native Element:
> Lest from this flying Steed unrein'd, (as once
> *Bellerophon*, though from a lower Clime)
> Dismounted, on the *Aleian* Field I fall
> Erroneous there to wander and forlorn.   (7.12–20)

The poet thus characterizes his daring enterprise once again: now that he, presumptuous in his imaginative flight, has soared all the way up to the Heavens to recount the cataclysmic battle between the forces of Satan and God, he asks for a safe return to earth, since he is about to begin his narrative of the Creation. And so he depends upon a celestial being or power (the Christian "meaning, not the Name I call" [7.5], says Milton in reference to Urania) to guide him, for the inspired poem, we have seen, is not solely his own creation. The mythic reference to the classical Bellerophon's presumptuous (and disastrous) flight to heaven upon the winged Pegasus gives greater resonance to the drama of the poet's own ambitious epic flight, which exceeds that of Bellerophon, and to his anxieties about its attendant perils: if he falls, after all, it will not be "from a lower clime," since he dares in *Paradise Lost* to soar "Above the flight of *Pegasean* wing" (7.4).

The poet's prominent voice, however, not only heightens the unusual and intense autobiographical dimension of *Paradise Lost*: its presence also helps to direct the reader's responses to a vast and complex narrative. There Milton frequently intervenes to comment on, criticize, or expose characters and events. Thus, for example, the poet sharply comments on the implications of Satan's deception of Uriel in Book 3 (the protean Satan has disguised himself as a cherub in order to inquire about "the happy seat of Man" [632]):

> So spake the false dissembler unperceiv'd;
> For neither Man nor Angel can discern
> Hypocrisy, the only evil that walks
> Invisible, except to God alone.   (681–4)

Milton avoids excessively idealizing angels here: as Milton notes in his *Christian Doctrine* (see YP 6:348) and dramatizes in his poem, there are many things his good angels do not know and understand. By unmasking Satan (the poet calls him "the fraudulent Imposter foul" a few lines later), Milton not only suggests the limited perception of his angels, but underscores how easily hypocrisy can go undetected, especially when Uriel is considered "The sharpest-sighted Spirit of all in Heav'n" (3.691). Satan's disguise demonstrates how easily "Hypocrisie turns himself into divers shapes," as Milton's contemporary Gerrard Winstanley observed, "yea, sometimes into an Angel of light" (*Works*, ed. G. Sabine [1941], p. 174; echoing 2 Cor. 11:14). And given how easily hypocrisy can beguile even the most discerning angel or human, the poet's intrusive comment prepares the reader to understand the danger and challenge facing Adam and Eve.

Similarly, the poet's critical response to Satan's long soliloquy on Mount Niphates (4.114ff.) adjusts the reader's perspective, sharply exposing the theatrical and potentially tragic Satan, prototype of all who would use a spiritual demeanor to conceal malicious motives, as an "Artificer of fraud . . . the first / That practis'd falsehood under saintly show." Milton recognizes the rhetorical power and emotional appeal of his own literary creation – especially a character who can speak with such dramatic force as he reveals his inward conflicts (see section 10) – and must warn the reader not to let him or herself become seduced by Satan's impressive performance beneath which lies "Deep malice." The narrator's intrusive responses attempt, at such moments, to contain the Satanic energies of his poem. Indeed, after his second soliloquy, in which Satan justifies his imperialistic enterprise – the pursuit of "Honor and Empire" enlarged "with revenge" and hatred which motivate him to conquer "this new World" and its inhabitants (4.389–92) – the narrator's voice once again intervenes. His commentary radically redefines for the reader Satan's motives in terms of political tyranny and Machiavellian behavior: "So spake the Fiend, and with necessity, / The Tyrant's plea, excus'd his devilish deeds" (4.393–4).

One of the poet's most intense warnings against seductive rhetoric occurs in response to Belial's speech during the council in Hell; just before he speaks, the poet puts his rhetorical performance in perspective for the reader:

> he seem'd
> For dignity compos'd and high exploit:
> But all was false and hollow; though his Tongue
> Dropt Manna, and could make the worse appear
> The better reason ...   (2.110ff.)

Milton has a keen ear for slick rhetoric and for political posturing. Given his own extensive rhetorical training, he could certainly admire a good rhetorical performance; but he also sensed how the arts of persuasion may be dangerously exploited. The poet's words remind the reader to be wary – to watch out for smooth words which please the ear, disguising (as in this case) the speaker's "low" thoughts (2.115). Like Satan or Milton's Comus, Belial speaks "glozing" words (*Comus*, 161; cf. *PL* 9.549) which may easily disarm his listeners. Belial does go on to give what appears to be some of the most sensible advice in the infernal council: arguing against pursuing war, he recognizes that there is little the devils can accomplish (except "worse" suffering) by pursuing their revenge and resisting God with force or guile. As soon as he has had his say, the narrator again warns us that "*Belial* with words cloth'd in reason's garb / Counsell'd ignoble ease, and peaceful sloth, / Not peace" (2.226–8). Indeed, the poet himself, in his sharp condemnation of Belial's polished rhetoric, offers the reader a model of discrimination as he distinguishes "sloth" from "peace."

Elsewhere when the poet intervenes with a warning voice, he does so with the profoundest sympathy for our first parents and their impending danger. The dramatic opening to Book 4 characterizes Satan as the great Dragon of Revelation and invokes "that warning voice" heard by St. John (Rev. 12:12):

> *Woe to the inhabitants on Earth!* that now,
> While time was, our first Parents had been warn'd
> The coming of thir secret foe, and scap'd
> Haply so scap'd his mortal snare.   (4.5–8)

The poet's personal and engaged response here is striking. One of intense feeling for the plight of humankind, it underscores a powerful sense of urgency, highlighting not only the *furor* and hatred driving Satan's Antichristian quest for revenge but also (and in complete contrast to Satan) the innocence of "frail man" (11). So too in Book 9, as Eve goes off on her own, the poet's personal voice bursts in: "O much deceiv'd, much failing, hapless *Eve*, / Of thy presum'd return! event perverse!" (404–5). Such a lamentation heightens the sense of tragedy and signals again the poet's sympathy as well as his sense of distress – his inability to disengage his personal response from his momentous narration of the Fall, the tragedy leading to "all our woe." Sometimes, however, the narrator's dramatic voice can seem much harsher, as when he laments during the devils' council (2.496–505) the terrible human discord and strife which have wasted the earth, a passage that looks forward to the dispiriting prophecy of human history at the end of *Paradise Lost*.

Other emotional reactions from the poet underscore the unfortunate nature of the Fall and the bliss of Edenic sexuality (see e.g. 4.773–5), poignantly reminding us of what we have irretrievably lost. Thus, in Book 5 the narrator describes the naked, innocent Eve ministering to Adam and their angelic guest:

>   in those hearts
> Love unlibidinous reign'd, nor jealousy
> Was understood, the injur'd Lover's Hell.   (448–50)

Moreover, in Book 8, just after we learn that Eve prefers that Adam (rather than the angel Raphael) tell her about philosophical matters because he will "solve high dispute / With conjugal Caresses," the poet interjects the following wistful rhetorical question: "O when meet now / Such pairs, in Love and mutual Honor join'd?" (55–8). Here, Milton reminds his readers that the Fall was by no means a *felix culpa* or "fortunate fall"; his response simultaneously underscores the poignancy of imagining the world of prelapsarian eroticism from a fallen perspective which the intrusive poet, though prophetically inspired, does indeed share with us.

A few examples can illustrate how the poet's narrative comments, even brief and seemingly unintrusive ones, are also crucial in guiding the reader's critical evaluation of the temptation itself as it unfolds in Book 9. Thus, after the first time Satan as serpent addresses Eve, using the seductive language of Petrarchan love poetry, the poet inserts his own brief comment, observing that Eve was "Not unamaz'd" (9.552). This double negative lets the reader know that while she is clearly impressed by this anomaly of the talking snake, her reason continues to operate. Yet after the serpent's clever autobiographical narrative, in which he demonstrates the miraculous power of the fruit, we hear again from the narrator who now notes that Eve was "Yet more amaz'd" (9.614), a comment indicating that she is indeed beginning to accept the serpent's arguments, even as she suspects his "overpraising." And as the temptation continues and Satan marshals his rhetorical powers to further his bold design, the narrator inserts a crucial qualification by reminding the reader that Eve is "yet sinless" (9.659) – and so she remains until she actually eats the forbidden fruit.

The narrator's responses and language also enable us to gauge the emotional and psychological transformations of our primal mother and father after the tragedy of the Fall. The devastating effects of their fall are registered by the powerful but inconclusive passage which brings Book 9 to a close:

> Thus they in mutual accusation spent
> The fruitless hours, but neither self-condemning,
> And of thir vain contest appear'd no end.

The poet's formal lines underscore the maze-like hopelessness of the inner Hell which Adam and Eve have brought upon themselves.

The narrator's tone and words, however, are remarkably different at the very end of Book 10. There his language (beginning with "they forthwith to the place / Repairing where he judg'd them prostrate fell / Before him reverent . . ." [1098–104]) explicitly repeats – without any criticism or qualification – the language of the newly penitent Adam only a few lines earlier: "What better can we do, than to the place / Repairing where he judg'd us, prostrate fall / Before him reverent . . ." (1086–92). By this point in the poem we have witnessed the painful reconciliation of Adam and Eve, heroically initiated by Eve herself. The poet's moving response, which looks forward to the end of the poem, thus measures the emotional and psychological distance between their bitter accusations at the end of Book 9 and their contrition at the end of Book 10. And in doing so, it also reinforces a newly found sense of community which now exists between the fallen narrator of *Paradise Lost* and our original mother and father.

9 Answerable styles

Highly self-conscious of the demanding genre he is undertaking and revising, Milton is aware of employing that "answerable style" (9.20) most suitable or equal to his inspired task. This may often involve writing in the rhetorically elevated or high style associated with the epic. Yet it should be said at the outset that there is no single style in *Paradise Lost*. Milton employs a variety of answerable styles to suit the rich variety of the poem itself, as subsequent sections of this volume will make even clearer. When Milton writes his hexaemeral epic in Book 7, for example, he appropriately uses Biblical diction, often closely echoing Genesis itself, to describe the dynamic process of the Creation (see section 17); or when he attempts to convey the bitter tones and colloquial diction of Adam and Eve's dispute after the Fall, the poet's own "alter'd style" (9.1132) notably avoids the grandeur of the epic high style characteristic of other parts of the poem (for example, its opening heroic books). The last books of the poem, with their frequently harrowing vision of postlapsarian human history, become increasingly austere and unadorned in their poetic style (they have fewer of Milton's famous epic similes, discussed below), which corresponds to their bleaker subject matter (see section 19). Elsewhere Milton even employs a mock-heroic style. By examining a selection of passages, we can begin to appreciate some of the more distinctive linguistic and syntactical features of the answerable styles in *Paradise Lost*.

Let us look for a moment again at the opening lines of *Paradise Lost*, an impressive example of Milton's poetic high style; the first six lines immediately convey the solemn grandeur and density with which Milton announces the sacred themes of his great epic narrative:

Of Man's First Disobedience, and the Fruit
Of that Forbidden Tree, whose mortal taste
Brought Death into the World, and all our woe,
With loss of *Eden*, till one greater Man
Restore us, and regain the blissful Seat,
Sing Heav'nly Muse . . .

Here the poet's suspended and inverted syntax – the separation of the genitive objects ("Of Man's First Disobedience, and the Fruit") at the beginning from the predicate by crucial subordinate clauses and other qualifying details elaborating the poem's major themes of disobedience, loss, woe, and restoration – contributes to the rhetorically elevated style of Miltonic epic. By delaying the main verb, *Sing*, until the beginning of line six, Milton creates a sense of suspension: the suspended syntax enables him to amplify the magnitude of his poem's sacred subject and the ambitious scope of his "advent'rous Song," its visionary performance taking us back in time to the first Adam, while looking forward to the Second Coming of Christ. Indeed, Milton's long and dense opening sentence, with its elaborate syntax, does not come to a full stop until line 16: it is more than twice as long as the opening sentence of the *Aeneid*. (Such long sentences, with multiple subordinate clauses, are a common feature of the poem's style and not necessarily unEnglish.) Its flexible yet controlled structure enables Milton to achieve an astonishing sense of concentration, as well as lucidity, with each precise qualification added incrementally within the poem's first twenty-six lines; in so doing, he highlights its central sacred themes, along with his own sense of soaring and perilous ambition, as we began to see in sections 7 and 8.

Or consider the narrator's sentence describing Satan's mighty fall from Heaven:

> Him the Almighty Power
> Hurl'd headlong flaming from th' Ethereal Sky
> With hideous ruin and combustion down
> To bottomless perdition, there to dwell
> In Adamantine Chains and penal Fire,
> Who durst defy th' Omnipotent to Arms.   (1.44–9)

Here again we begin with a distinctive Miltonic inversion of the natural word order: object, subject, verb. The effect of this particular syntactical arrangement, with its dislocation of conventional English syntax, is to convey immense force and violence (especially when Milton stresses the word "Hurl'd" at the beginning of line 45), and to enhance God's agency, while reducing Satan to a mere object catapulted through space. Thus Milton enables us to sense the awesome power of God, which we will see in Book 6, as well as the Titanic scale of the conflict in Heaven which led to Satan's fiery punishment in Hell and to his subsequent quest for revenge. The qualifying prepositional phrase, "With hideous ruin and combustion," likewise conveys the violent disturbance of that great cosmic war and fall fuelled by Satan's fierce defiance of the Almighty. Similarly, the "bottomless perdition" to which Satan is hurled ("perdition" being derived from the Latin *perdere*, to lose or to destroy) suggests not only great destruction and loss, but also a location dynamic in its ongoing displacement ("bottomless") and reflective of the fallen angel's progressively deeper spiritual damnation. The poet's precise language and inflected syntax in this passage – the word arrangement here makes good poetic sense, as we have seen – thus effectively convey the character and consequences of those superhuman forces at war in the world of his visionary epic.

A brief look at the end of the poem can illustrate how Milton employs a high style before modulating, in the latter part of Book 11 and for much of Book 12, to a less elevated style suited to Michael's sober account of human history after the Fall. When the archangel takes Adam up the hill of Paradise to begin the vision of history, we first get a most impressive heroic catalogue of exotic empires:

from the destin'd Walls
Of *Cambalu*, seat of *Cathaian Can*.
And *Samarchand* by *Oxus*, *Temir's* Throne,
To *Paquin* of *Sinaean* Kings, and thence
To *Agra* and *Lahor* of great *Mogul*
. . .

Rich *Mexico* the seat of *Montezume*,
And *Cusco* in *Peru*, the richer seat
Of *Atabalipa*, and yet unspoil'd
Guiana . . .

(11.387–410)

Among the last examples of the high style in *Paradise Lost*, this stunning roll-call of place-names, reminding us of the great catalogue of fallen angels in Book 1 (376ff.), conveys a sense of earthly power, glory, and magnificence before shifting our attention to more internal sights. After all, Milton's radical Protestant poem, with its austere last two books, is ultimately about "nobler sights" (11.411) – sights more spiritual and less worldly than the great civilizations and imperial power valorized by more traditional national and martial epics. And so when the poem subsequently launches into its prophetic account of the misdeeds and tribulations of human history from Adam to the Apocalypse, it no longer indulges in glorious epic catalogues (compare the shocking catalogue of diseases: 11.477ff.) or displays the elevated epic style suitable to heroic sections of the poem like Books 1 and 2 (compare the plain Biblical paraphrase characterizing Michael's narration of Abraham in Book 12:128ff.).

Now consider in contrast to Milton's high ceremonious or elevated style, his effective use of the mock-heroic style in a passage like this from Book 7, where the archangel Raphael describes the creation of the animals and other living creatures:

First crept
The Parsimonious Emmet, provident
Of future, in small room large heart enclos'd,
Pattern of just equality perhaps
Hereafter, join'd in her popular Tribes
Of Commonalty.

(7.484–9)

Here Milton uses a gigantic word – "Parsimonious" – to characterize a tiny creature, the ant: this incongruous use of big words to describe small things is essentially mock-heroic (that ironically grand style perfected by Restoration and eighteenth-century English poets). It amusingly conveys the paradoxical nature of this very small creature with its "large heart." For indeed the little emmet, among all the living creatures, does become a kind of Miltonic hero in the poem, emblematic of political "equality" itself. As his use of the mock-heroic illustrates, Milton can greatly vary his style within the epic – it is not consistently grand. Even at the end of Book 1, after describing the building of the magnificent Pandemonium, Milton shifts to a mock-heroic style as he likens the thronging rebel angels first to huge giants, then to "smallest Dwarfs," and then to "Faery Elves" either seen or dreamt by a "belated Peasant" (see 1.777ff.). The poet is playing with size here and even taunting and belittling the devils with the punning phrase "at large": "Thus incorporeal Spirits to smallest forms / Reduc'd thir shapes immense, and were at large." The mock-heroic comparisons render the exalted stature of the rebel angels ambiguous.

Another particularly revealing example of the way Milton varies and contrasts style in the poem occurs in Book 10, where he juxtaposes the responses of Adam and Eve to the Son who has descended from Heaven to judge them. The difference here between Adam's fallen style and Eve's is striking. Adam responds first to the Son in a defensive speech of accusation (implicating God) that goes on for nineteen lines. Indeed, the suspended syntax of his second long sentence reinforces his own ignoble evasion as he blames Eve, rather than himself, for their recent transgression: "This Woman whom thou mad'st to be my help, / . . . thy perfet gift . . . so Divine, / That from her hand I could suspect no ill, / . . . Shee gave me of the Tree, and I did eat" (10.137–43). Eve's response to the Son, in contrast, consists of only one line: "The Serpent me beguil'd and I did eat" (10.162). There is no bluster here, no attempt to hide what happened, and no self-serving attempt to blame Adam; and there is no suspended syntax: Eve uses simple Biblical diction as her language echoes Genesis 3:13. The "answerable style" and phrasing she employs in her fallen response are thus much closer to Scripture, a detail that would seem significant to the fit Protestant reader of Milton's sacred poem. Her Biblical-style response, moreover, anticipates her

self-sacrificing heroism which proves so crucial in effecting the reconciliation between our first parents (see section 18).

Sometimes Milton can be particularly effective in shaping sentence structure or syntax to imitate meaning. A notable instance
occurs in Book 2 as the faltering Satan is just about to begin his
solitary voyage through vast Chaos (910–20): the sentence's opening phrase, "Into this wild Abyss," is immediately followed not by
the subject and a main verb of motion such as "leapt" (as we might
expect), but by six lines (911–16) describing the confusion and wildness of Chaos. Then Milton repeats the opening phrase and continues the sentence: "Into this wild Abyss the wary fiend / Stood on the
brink of Hell and look'd a while, / Pondering his Voyage" (917–19).
Indeed, Milton's particular choice of verb – "Stood" – conveys the
hesitation of the wary Satan standing before Chaos (rather than a
heroic or bold beginning to his epic journey), as does the repetition
and suspension Milton employs in the sentence structure itself.

Certainly one of the most distinctive and brilliant stylistic features of the poem is Milton's frequent and striking use of epic or
extended similes with their elaborate and complex comparisons.
This is another technique of poetic craftsmanship by which Milton
alerts his reader to the fact that he is writing an epic, even as he
revises the ambitious genre and rivals the ancient models stylisti-
cally. In a poem like the *Iliad*, the epic or long simile is always vivid,
its metaphors drawn from the everyday and (often violent) natural
world to register and explore the emotions and often terrifying experiences associated with warfare and death (for example, regiments
of troops are compared to innumerable bees issuing from a crevice;
Hector furiously attacking the Greeks is compared to a pitiless lion
coming down upon cattle; Achilles swiftly pursuing Hector is compared to a screaming hawk swooping upon a dove; etc.). Virgil too
will use long similes to give a sense of immediacy and emotional
power to the conflict between Empire and Eros in his *Aeneid*. In Book
4.441–9, to take one famous instance, the emotional and spiritual
struggle of pious Aeneas in Carthage, whose mind remains unmoved
by Dido's tearful pleas, is conveyed by the poet's simile of a stout oak
tree blasted by northern Alpine winds which shake its trunk and
scatter its high branches as the oak still clings to the rocks.

In *Paradise Lost* Milton draws upon a large variety of subjects for his many epic similes (they are especially numerous in the first two books): the natural world, Biblical and classical history and myth, pastoral life, husbandry, city life, science, Renaissance exploration, eastern tyranny, among other subjects. These expanded similes are essential passages in the poem and never merely digressive or decorative. Nor are they, like Homer's similes, usually stylized and brilliant vignettes that tend "to hold the narrative in suspended animation at a certain moment" (Silk, *The Iliad*, p. 60). In *Paradise Lost*, they are carefully integrated into the poem: their precise, sharp, and evocative details provide valuable commentary on the narrative, prompting us as readers to engage in the active and discriminating process of interpreting character and action; here, for example, is the first heroic simile, which depicts the size of the fallen Satan:

> his other Parts besides
> Prone on the Flood, extended long and large
> Lay floating many a rood, in bulk as huge
> As whom the Fables name of monstrous size,
> *Titanian*, or *Earth-born*, that warr'd on *Jove*,
> *Briareos* or *Typhon*, whom the Den
> By ancient *Tarsus* held, or that Sea-beast
> *Leviathan* . . .   (1.194ff.)

After we have just seen an example of Satan's powerful rhetoric, as he plays the role of the inspired military leader encouraging his fallen troops to resist a tyrannical God, this long epic simile enables us to consider carefully Satan's size. The "tenor" here, in literary critical terms, is Satan stretched out on the burning lake, while the "vehicle" is the catalogue of terrible mythic monsters; the point of likeness between them is their awesome hugeness. But how huge exactly is left to our critical discretion, since the repetition of the conjunction "or" invites us to consider a series of alternatives including huge mythic monsters (Typhon was serpent-headed) who rebelled against Zeus; the Leviathan, of course, invites us to compare Satan to the Biblical sea monster of Job 41 and "the crooked serpent" of Isaiah 27:1. Indeed, as the epic comparison continues (201ff.), it focuses our attention on the theme of deception: Milton describes a Norwegian sea-pilot who in the midst of night mistakes the Leviathan monster for an island by whose side he can moor his ship. The simile's story warns us to be on the alert as we read Milton's complex poem – to probe beneath the surface of the epic's narrative and drama, and not to be taken in by Satan's devilish cunning and protean appearances. A passage like this, moreover, complicates our perspective on the majesty and nobility of the heroic Satan highlighted in the early books of the poem (see section 10).

Or take the following simile from Book 2 as a commentary on the vast scope of Satan's daring journey and its imperial designs. Satan's "solitary flight" as he heads towards the Gates of Hell evokes the world of Renaissance commercial exploration:

> As when far off at Sea a Fleet descri'd
> Hangs in the Clouds, by *Equinoctial* Winds
> Close sailing from *Bengala*, or the Isles
> Of *Ternate* and *Tidore*, whence Merchants bring
> Thir spicy Drugs: they on the Trading Flood
> Through the wide *Ethiopian* to the Cape
> Ply stemming nightly toward the Pole.   (2.636–42)

Besides evoking a sense of vast distance (a common effect in *Paradise Lost*), the simile places Satan's adventurous journey in a Renaissance mercantile context that we have not yet seen in the poem. Here, Milton compares Satan to a commercial voyager on a mission to bring home exotic treasure. Indeed, the "spicy Drugs" suggest the savory smell of the desired but forbidden fruit that Satan will use to tempt Eve in Book 9 (and in that sense the simile functions proleptically by foreshadowing later events). Milton's simile refers to the world of exploration that had helped to establish and expand European empires in the Renaissance – including the Portuguese empire whose colonial ambitions are recounted in Camoens' nationalistic epic, *The Lusiads* (1572). And so Satan himself is viewed momentarily in terms of the early modern European commercial conquerors. In this way, Milton's poem, which is continually subverting and revising traditional epic values, manages to associate Satan's daring enterprise and individualism with both the enterprise of Renaissance commercialism and the European epic famous for celebrating it.

Another Miltonic simile illustrates how *Paradise Lost* evokes the world of early modern science to raise larger questions about the nature of knowledge and perception. Here is the simile Milton uses when Satan lands on the orb of the sun in Book 3:

> There lands the Fiend, a spot like which perhaps
> Astronomer in the Sun's lucent Orb
> Through his glaz'd Optic Tube yet never saw.   (3.588–90)

Milton's lines refer to Galileo's famous discovery of the sun spots in 1609: the simile, with its allusion to contemporary scientific knowledge, gives *Paradise Lost* as epic a modern quality. We know from *Areopagitica* that Milton met and admired the old, blind Galileo – the daring revolutionary scientist who had engaged in a new kind of free inquiry. And yet these lines in *Paradise Lost* are hedged by qualification: the comparison of Satan to a sun spot introduces uncertainties about the nature of new scientific knowledge itself. The hesitant phrasing in line 588 – "a spot like which perhaps" – coupled with the phrase "yet never saw" in line 590, suggests that Milton's view of such exciting new knowledge remains ambivalent: it is Satan, after all, who will later tell Eve about turning his thoughts "to Speculations high or deep" as he considers "all things visible" in the cosmos (9.602ff.). A later simile comparing the unclouded vision of the angel Raphael with the "less assur'd" vision of Galileo (5.261ff.) likewise suggests the poet's ambivalence about the pursuit of human knowledge which attempts to aspire much too high, a theme developed in Book 8 when Raphael discusses with Adam the nature of the universe (see section 17).

One final example – an unusually complicated one – can illustrate how Milton exploits the poetic technique of the epic simile during the temptation scene of Book 9. Here is how Milton describes the tempter as he is about to address Eve for the last time:

> As when of old some Orator renown'd
> In *Athens* or free *Rome*, where Eloquence
> Flourish'd, since mute, to some great cause addrest,
> Stood in himself collected, while each part,
> Motion, each act won audience ere the tongue,
> Sometimes in highth began, as no delay
> Of Preface brooking through his Zeal of Right.   (670–6)

What makes this passage particularly complex is that Milton develops comparisons simultaneously. This extended simile has more than one vehicle: Satan is being compared to an accomplished classical rhetorician, as well as to an actor. The word "part" suggests, among other meanings (e.g. "part of the body" or even "moral act"), that Satan is playing a theatrical role. And the word "motion" suggests not only "gesture" and "persuasive force," but also a "puppet-show," a meaning Milton has in mind when he refers to "a meer artificiall *Adam* . . . an Adam as he is in the motions" in the passage from *Areopagitica* which we examined in section 3. The theatrical meaning is reinforced even further by the sense of "act" as a dramatic performance. In this way, Milton's complex simile operates on more than one level, giving us a full sense of the guileful rhetorical powers and theatrical performance Satan employs in his last temptation speech – the speech that finally persuades the allured Eve to taste the forbidden fruit.

Jonathan Richardson, one of Milton's early biographers, aptly observed that "a Reader of *Milton* must be Always upon Duty; he is Surrounded with Sense, it rises in every Line, every Word is to the Purpose; There are no Lazy Intervals, All has been Consider'd, and Demands, and Merits Observation" (*Early Lives*, p. 315). Richardson's perceptive observation could of course apply to many aspects of *Paradise Lost*: its poetic concentration and subtlety, its intellectual and sensuous richness, its stylistic variety and expressiveness – all these features require a particularly alert, engaged, and discriminating reader. It is a comment that applies especially well to Milton's carefully wrought similes (we have considered only a few notable examples) with their brilliant and precise details – passages of particular poetic density that challenge us as active readers to discern their complex comparisons and meanings with special care and to relate those meanings to the larger contexts and concerns of his vast unfolding narrative of disobedience, loss, and restoration.

10 Satan: daring ambition and heroic ideology

The opening books of *Paradise Lost* bring out the rich complexity of Milton's Satan – both his attractiveness and his perversity. As Milton portrays this cosmic adversary (the meaning of his Hebraic name), the enemy of God and man, the poet reveals the ambiguities of Satan's heroic self-assertion, as well as the aggression manifested by his martial values and his unyielding defiance. A figure of immense passion and energy, Satan appears as a courageous and charismatic military leader capable of arousing his fallen legions. He is, moreover, a remarkably skillful rhetorician. Like other epic heroes – for example, Achilles in the *Iliad* or the raging, vengeful Turnus in the *Aeneid* – he is also characterized by his great wrath. Yet Satan manages to discipline this epic *furor*, marshalling it in order to pursue what the Romantic critic, William Hazlitt, so aptly called his "daring ambition." Indeed, such Romantic commentators as Blake, Shelley, and Byron especially admired Satan's energy and "sublime grandeur" (Shelley's phrase), portraying him as the hero of *Paradise Lost*. But insofar as Milton's Satan appears magnificently heroic and displays "fierce passions" (to borrow another of Hazlitt's apt phrases), his martial values are by and large those of the classical epic hero. These values and this outmoded heroic ideology Milton's poem puts under considerable scrutiny and often subverts. Furthermore, the poem shows us that Satan is also perverse: he has defiantly turned away from his divine creator, forcefully asserting that he is "self-begot, self-rais'd / By [his] own quick'ning power" (5.860–1).

Satan seems impressive partly because he asserts, as he addresses his fallen legions in Hell, the power of his mind to transform thoroughly his environment: "The mind is its own place, and in itself / Can make a Heav'n of Hell, a Hell of Heav'n" (1.254–5). The rhetorical figure of speech in line 255 – chiasmus – reminds us that the active, heroic Satan of Milton's poem does indeed speak as a forceful and exciting rhetorician. His fixed mind, he insists, is not to be "chang'd by Place or Time" (253): here we see the sheer willfulness of Satan, his hardness of mind, his refusal to repent. This is the same willfulness which lies behind his rebellious claim in Heaven that he is "self-begot," that his puissance is completely self-generated, and that he is, in effect, wholly the creator of his own identity, which enables him to act altogether apart from God. Thus while Milton's Satan is indeed theologically perverse, the early books of the poem brilliantly enable us to feel his power and appeal.

There Satan does indeed seem splendid in defeat. We are meant to notice the militant Satan's extraordinary courage, defiance, and pride:

> What though the field be lost?
> All is not lost; the unconquerable Will,
> And study of revenge, immortal hate,
> And courage never to submit or yield:
> And what is else not to be overcome?
> That Glory never shall his wrath or might
> Extort from me.

These lines, from the first speech we hear Satan deliver in Hell (1.105–11), express his fierce determination not to be overcome: he will marshal his forces to continue his rebellion against an arbitrary tyrant and irrational power, which is how he portrays God. What motivates Satan is an intense and unyielding hatred, a sense of injured merit, and the desire for revenge. Milton's poem enables us to admire Satan's martial bravery and individualism, including his willingness to take exceptional risks, while allowing us to see the destructive, self-aggrandizing motives which fuel his vaunting behavior and unrelenting drive. What Satan the general refuses to give up here, moreover, is a pagan hero's notion of individual glory, which he pursues at all costs. Speaking with the pride, rage, and vengefulness of an Achilles, he reveals his pagan sensibility – his aggression and values resembling those of the combative, daring warrior of classical epic. But Milton further complicates and revises this heroic portrait when, just after this bold speech, he comments on Satan's "pain," his "Vaunting aloud" though "rackt with deep despair" (125–6). While the theatrical and rhetorical Satan projects an image of a powerful, willful leader – one who has impressively disciplined his great energies and rage – the poet focuses our attention on Satan's inner torment, warning us not to be taken in by his forceful rhetoric and alerting us to the incongruity between outward performance and inward despair. As we shall see later, such inwardness gives Satan's character greater complexity and depth.

The first two books of *Paradise Lost*, which most closely resemble pagan epic, especially highlight the heroic dimensions and dramatic appeal of Satan. We see him as an experienced and inspired military leader majestically rousing his stunned and weary troops who, once they assume their impressive martial formations and godlike stature, do indeed seem to surpass all the heroes and armies of history and legend (see 1.573–89). Nor does Milton make his heroic Satan, with his "mighty Stature" (1.222), a physically unattractive or grotesque figure: his Satan, unlike the more popular conception of the Devil, has no horns and tail, no hump and cloven feet, no great physical deformity (except that the lines of his face were scarred by lightning). Although hurled headlong flaming from Heaven to Hell (and having fallen for nine days), the towering Satan, once one of God's archangels "great in Power" (5.660), still exudes a sense of divine energy and splendor in the poem's early books, since "his form had yet not lost / All her Original brightness" (1.591–2; cf. 10.450ff.). Nor does the warlike Satan, despite his steadfast hatred, lack feeling for his vanquished compatriots for whom he shows "Signs of remorse and passion" (1.605).

Satan's great speech of acceptance (2.430ff.), once it is determined that he is the one to make the hazardous epic journey through Chaos to earth in order to conquer or destroy man's paradisal world, is a shrewd example of political rhetoric and manipulation: the rising monarch, fearing rivals, prudently "prevented all reply," the poet tells us. But it is also a speech in which Satan displays his heroic character and, without an indication of selfish motives, expresses his willingness to risk his own safety and go it alone "Through all the Coasts of dark destruction" as he seeks deliverance for his suffering compatriots. Satan's self-sacrifice parallels that of the Son's in Book 3 and indeed, after his speech, Satan assumes a new godlike stature (2.477ff.). His epic journey, like the stoic Aeneas' in search of a new Troy, will be "hard," though Satan (who lacks Aeneas' *pietas*) will prove himself to be a more active heroic figure than his more passive, fate-driven Virgilian model. His odyssey or voyage, which he makes "Undaunted" (2.955) through the warring elements of Chaos, is even more dangerous than the voyages of Ulysses and Jason's Argonauts (2.1016ff.). Indeed, Satan's daring leadership assumes various manifestations: he resembles a savior and liberator on a heroic and romantic quest to free his comrades from "this dark and dismal house of pain" (2.823) and to regain Jerusalem; a Mosaic deliverer wandering through the wilderness on the way to the Promised Land; a political revolutionary freeing his compatriots from "servitude inglorious" (9.141; cf. 10.368ff.); a daring voyager on an adventurous expedition to find and possess new and better lands (4.935ff.) or search out new worlds.

One way, however, that Milton conveys the equivocal nature of Satan's heroic appeal and nobility is by evoking both the tyrannical and exotic world of the east: as a warring political leader, Satan also resembles an Asiatic despot, a "great Sultan" conducting his forces (1.347ff.). Or at the beginning of Book 2, we see him in all his splendor on the raised throne of Pandemonium:

> High on a Throne of Royal State, which far
> Outshone the wealth of *Ormus* and of *Ind*,
> Or where the gorgeous East with richest hand
> Show'rs on her Kings *Barbaric* Pearl and Gold,
> Satan exalted sat, by merit rais'd
> To that bad eminence.   (2.1–6)

This evocative passage may remind us that the great power and opulence associated with eastern kingdoms, including Ormuz in the Persian Gulf and especially India itself, was the subject of another famous European epic – Camoens' *Lusiads*, the imperialistic epic of Portugal commemorating the daring voyage of Vasco da Gama to India. The imperial Satan of Milton's epic also pursues glory, renown, and dominion; and later in the poem Milton compares him to commercial sea voyagers associated with European empires (2.636–42). Here at the beginning of Book 2, Milton's evocation of eastern power and wealth both elevates Satan – his magnificence and power exceed those of these rich and exotic kingdoms – and explodes his dazzling display of royal authority, especially when the poet inserts the word "*Barbaric*" in line 4. (Note that the syntactical suspension here – the delay of subject and verb until line 5 – likewise contributes to the sense of pomp and grandeur which Milton deflates.) Milton, moreover, is already implying a contrast not only with God "High Thron'd above all highth" (3.58), but also with the Son whom we will soon meet in the next book: the Son himself is raised by "Merit" (3.309), though of an entirely different sort from Satan's – not merit defined in terms of aristocratic or imperialistic ideals of honor, but merit defined in terms of voluntary service to God.

If Milton's portrait of the martial and magnificent Satan owes much to the outmoded heroic code and ideology we associate with imperialistic and ancient epic (see also section 16), his portrait of the regal Satan, with his "Monarchal pride" (2.428) and "pomp

Supreme" (2.510), owes much to the poet's political tracts in which he scrutinized and attacked the politics and art of tyrannical power. Indeed, one of Milton's early biographers, John Toland, suggested that "the chief design" of *Paradise Lost* is "to display the different Effects of Liberty and Tyranny" (*Brief Lives*, p. 182). In his anti-monarchical tracts and his *Defenses of the English People*, Milton presented the political tyrant as boundless in his will and arbitrary in his use of power; with his "brute will" he pursues "his glory" (YP 3:204), as well as hateful revenge. Tyranny, which Milton saw as the outgrowth of earthly kingship, could become dangerously artful and equivocal: he warned of the "craft of the infuriated king" (YP 4:518), the skillful tyrant who employs "glozing words" and attempts "to counterfet Religious" (YP 3:582, 361), much as the protean and theatrical Satan of *Paradise Lost* might put on a "saintly show" (4.122) or use "Ambiguous words" (5.703) and "calumnious Art" (770) to promote his subversive political designs in Heaven. Where force will not work to further their designs, the monarch of Hell tells his compatriots, they may resort, Machiavellian-style, to "fraud or guile" (1.646; cf. 6.794–5).

Milton also associated royal forms of tyranny with idolatry: it is "a form of idolatry," he wrote in his *First Defense*, "to ask for a king who demands that he be worshipped and granted honors like those of a god" (YP 4:369); so in *Paradise Lost* Satan in his heavenly chariot (imitating the Son just as evil parodies good) becomes an "Idol of Majesty" (6.101). And so too Milton early in the poem deflates the heroic power and splendor of Satan's godlike rebel leaders by associating them with multiple forms of idolatry and false adoration (as well as lust and violence) in the lengthy epic catalogue of Book 1 (see lines 376–522). In his political tracts, Milton stressed the proud and rageful character of a tyrant, as well as the "unbridled passion" (YP 4:387) with which he exalts himself above the rest of mankind by proclaiming himself a god. A "proud / Aspirer" (6.89–90), the monarchic Satan of *Paradise Lost* himself clearly possesses such characteristics. In the case of Charles I, Milton believed that he was witnessing first-hand the horrors and dangers of political tyranny, and we can see that his mythic portrait of Satan owes something to Milton's contemporary political experiences.

But the difference is that Milton's proud Satan tends to be much more inward than the political writer's idolatrous tyrants and

earthly kings. It is the poet of *Paradise Lost*, after all, who dares
to explore the inner torment, restlessness, and grief of the political
tyrant. This is not to say that Milton wants his readers to sympathize
with tyranny; but he does give us a nuanced portrait of Satan and
his ambiguous political and heroic behavior, exploring his motives
for revenge and tyranny, while showing us his potential for tragic
feeling. Milton's tyrannical Satan may in some ways resemble the
historical Charles (or, rather, Milton's depiction of him), but in his
inwardness and despair he more closely resembles Shakespeare's
Macbeth. In this respect, too, Milton's Satan is a much more inward
character than one would expect to find, say, among the epic heroes
of Homer and Virgil (despite the depth of feeling Homer gives to the
suffering Achilles or the pathos Virgil gives his "pious" Aeneas):
these heroic individuals tend to be defined more exclusively by their
public and external achievements, actions, or status, and they never
speak dramatic soliloquies, as Satan does, as though he were alone
on a stage. By giving Satan such interiority, Milton further complicates and revises the heroic materials he inherits.

Satan's soliloquy on Mount Niphates (4.32–113), as he views
beautiful Eden for the first time, illustrates the unusual complexity
of Milton's portrait of God's great adversary. Here the poet develops
Satan's inner life, giving him psychological depth, including contradictory feelings and moods:

> O thou that with surpassing Glory crown'd,
> Look'st from thy sole Dominion like the God
> Of this new World; at whose sight all the Stars
> Hide thir diminisht heads; to thee I call,
> But with no friendly voice, and add thy name
> O Sun, to tell thee how I hate thy beams
> That bring to my remembrance from what state
> I fell, how glorious once above thy Sphere;
> Till Pride and worse Ambition threw me down
> Warring in Heav'n against Heav'n's matchless King:
> Ah wherefore! he deserv'd no such return
> From me, whom he created what I was
> In that bright eminence, and with his good
> Upbraided none; nor was his service hard.

The very fact that Milton gives his agonized Satan a long soliloquy (he has five in the poem: see also 4.358ff., 4.505ff., 9.99ff.,

9.473ff.) underscores the pathos and potential tragedy of his restless existence. After all, we associate the soliloquy with some of the
most memorable tragic protagonists and heroes of the Renaissance
stage – with Marlowe's Doctor Faustus or with Hamlet or Macbeth.
Milton clearly wants to heighten the dramatic power and passion of
his Satan (who begins "in sighs" and punctuates his soliloquy with
dramatic outbursts like "Ah wherefore!" and later "Me miserable!"
and "Ay me") and to make us *feel* what it is like to be a fallen creature, as Milton explores Satan's inner division, conflicts, anguish
and despair in this probing speech of self-revelation.

Satan's address to the sun is his own invocation to light; however,
this negative invocation differs sharply from Milton's in Book 3, for
the solitary Satan, unlike the poet, hates the light and the world
from which he feels so painfully excluded. Nevertheless, Satan con-
demns himself here: he acknowledges the goodness of his creator
(cf. 5.853ff. where he denies, with sophistry, that God is his creator
at all) and indeed admits that God did not deserve such ingratitude
from him, since the Father's service was by no means hard. These are
clearly different claims from Satan's more public defiance of God as
tyrannical and vengeful, characteristics more closely approximat-
ing Satan's own behavior. As the dramatic speech continues, Satan
begins to engage in a probing inner dialogue: "Hadst thou the same
free Will and Power to stand? / Thou hadst." And Satan reveals, often
with considerable acuity, his own sterility (69–70), that he himself
brought about his own fall (71–2), that his Hell and torments are
psychological and inward ("myself am Hell," 75ff.), and that if he
is supreme, he is so, paradoxically, only "In misery." Like Marlowe's
Faustus, Satan could repent (93ff.), but of course he will not since he
disdains the very idea of "submission" (what heavenly service now
becomes in the speech) and especially dreads, like a competitive epic
warrior, "shame." And so as the soliloquy moves towards its end,
Satan becomes more and more hardened and more and more set
upon his original course of revenge to soothe his "wounds of deadly
hate," asserting that any reconciliation with God, now imagined by
Satan as an oppressive Calvinist God or "punisher" (103), is impos-
sible and hopeless. The solipsistic Satan, having rejected his better
impulses and his feelings of remorse, concludes his theatrical speech
fully committed to evil and to the imperial ambitions (the "Divided

Empire" he will hold "with Heav'n's King") which has fueled his daring quest from Hell.

Satan's dramatic soliloquies do in fact become increasingly solipsistic, subjective, and inward: he goes from addressing the sun to addressing the earth (9.99ff.), the territory he aims to destroy, to addressing, in his last soliloquy, his "Thoughts" (9.473ff.). By this last speech, we no longer see Satan (as we did in his first soliloquy) debating in his mind his conflicting impulses; rather, here the furious and sexually deprived Satan is completely bent on his mission of revenge and destruction. The hot Hell always burning within him and his utter hatred of female beauty – for he has just been stunned by Eve's profound beauty, softness, and grace – prompt him to launch into this speech of misogyny in which he also expresses his contempt for man's material nature ("of limb / Heroic built, though of terrestrial mould"). Satan concludes that the only way for him to overcome the alarming power of female beauty is to approach it with "stronger hate": here the solipsistic Satan, now cunningly disguised as a serpent and revealing his "Hellish hate" (3.298), has come a long way from the magnificent vaunting epic-style general and Prince of Hell whose passion and heroic energies dominate the poem's early books; nor does the spiteful serpent-tempter of Adam and Eve resemble at this moment the great cosmic antagonist of God in the epic war in Heaven – he "who erst contended / With Gods to sit the highest" (9.163–4).

Another notable way Milton deflates Satan's heroic self-assertion and exposes the perversity of his "self-begot" powers is by including his remarkable encounter with the grotesque personifications of Sin and Death (2.648–870), who guard the gates of Hell and later build a "stupendous" bridge between Hell and the new world (10.229–409). In this unusual and suggestive episode, Milton, generally a nonallegorical writer (unlike, say, Spenser or Bunyan), resorts to allegory to explore the deeper nature of Satanic creation and evil: Satan's family members, Sin and Death, are personified, so that character embodies an abstract concept or quality (e.g. Despair in *The Faerie Queene* or Ignorance in *The Pilgrim's Progress*). Although he wears a kingly crown and shakes his "dreadful Dart," the terrifying, deformed, and shadowy figure of Death has no firm, constant shape or features, anticipating the fact that he will indeed assume many

dismal shapes after the Fall, as Adam painfully learns in Book 11;
moreover, his rage is a projection of Satan's own destructive wrath
against God and his creation. And Sin, partly based on Spenser's
Error in *The Faerie Queene* (Book 1.1.14ff.) – a fair woman to the
waist but a horrid serpent below – appears surrounded by monstrous Hell hounds who hideously bark as they gnaw her entrails
as their "repast," a perverse image of maternal nourishment and
Satanic appetite.

Although Satan fails to recognize them at first, Sin and Death
are the creations of his own perverse imagination, for Satan can
create only out of himself, a parody of, among other things, materialistic creation *ex deo* in the poem. Having been challenged by
furious Death in an epic-style confrontation – the poet refers to "the
mighty Combatants" and to the potential for "great deeds" – Satan
hears from Sin, who intervenes, an extraordinary account of the
monstrous family history of this infernal Trinity: Sin is both daughter and "wife" to Satan (with whom he had "dalliance" in Heaven),
and Death is their offspring. Sin's narrative further qualifies Satan's
heroic grandeur and romantic appeal as it reveals his appalling sexual life. Born from the head of Satan (whom Sin calls "my Author,"
2.864) in the midst of his conspiracy against God, Sin's birth parodies not only the birth of Athena from the head of Zeus, but also
the birth of Eve (from Adam's side) and the generation of the Son:
she is truly the creation of Satan's "proud imaginations" (2.10). It
is, moreover, a painful birth, underscoring the fact that, in Milton's
myth, Satan himself invents pain. His subsequent narcissistic and
incestuous relation with his daughter (in her he sees his "perfect image") results in yet another painful and particularly violent birth –
that of Death – which is then followed by the second incestuous
relation, the rape of Sin by her own son, which in turn begets the
proliferating Hell hounds tormenting Sin. And so sexual relations in
Satan's family are characterized by rape, incest, internal violation,
endless narcissism, shame, and unnatural pain – in striking contrast to the healthy prelapsarian sexuality of our first parents (see
section 14). This shocking allegorical episode, by no means "faulty"
and "unskilful" as Samuel Johnson complained, powerfully illustrates a number of points about Satanic existence and creation: that
Satanic evil is self-generating and self-consuming; that it involves

hatred for a prior creator (Death, after all, is both Sin's "Son and foe," just as Satan is God's enemy); that Satanic existence, desire, and appetite are indeed forever dissatisfied and unappeasable (the monstrous Hell hounds never give Sin "rest or intermission"); and that Satanic creation generates only incestuous images of its creator. Satan represents the negative creator in *Paradise Lost* – he is after all the "great Author" of Sin and Death (10.236) – and the fact that his perverse creations are allegorical highlights Milton's largely anti-allegorical bias as an epic poet.

We will have occasion later to examine Satan's equivocal political behavior and his rhetorical skills as the primal tempter (in sections 16 and 18), but let us look ahead for a moment to Book 10 where, for the last time, Satan seems heroic upon his triumphant return from his perilous epic adventure to the new world he has conquered. There he first joyfully meets Sin and Death, who applaud his "magnific deeds" and "Trophies" (354–5), and then, like an oriental despot (recalling the "great Sultan" of Book 1), he greets his "great consulting Peers" (456) in Pandemonium as they rise from "thir dark *Divan*" (457), the Turkish council of state: that description already qualifies the exultant heroism and nobility of his glorious reappearance in Hell, as does the deflating and mock-heroic phrase "false glitter" in line 452. Indeed, the unexpected response to his heroic victory speech proclaiming the success of his wondrous and daring exploits (in which he lies to his fellow devils, since neither Night nor Chaos opposed his arduous journey, as he asserts) is a "dismal universal hiss, the sound / Of public scorn" (10.508–10); and this is followed by Satan's Ovidian metamorphosis (10.511ff.) into a monstrous serpent – an essence he possessed from the very beginning of the poem (the "infernal Serpent," 1.34) – as he moves down the chain of being from speaking to hissing. The rest of the devils are themselves transformed into ugly serpents: resembling the apocalyptic Dragon of Revelation 12:9 and larger than Ovid's huge serpent Python, Satan is the most powerful and monstrous of them all. Given Satan's "foul descent" (9.163) into a serpent to entice Eve, the divine punishment and curse is indeed both ironic and appropriate. As a final curse, these snakes are tantalized: to aggravate them, God springs up a grove of trees with "fair Fruit," but the devils remain "parcht with scalding thirst and hunger fierce"

(10.547ff.) as the illusory fruit they eat – thinking it will satisfy their appetite – turns to "bitter Ashes." Their degraded actions at this moment recall the hungry and deceived Eve who, at the Fall, "knew not eating Death" (9.792).

At this point in the poem, Milton's narrative carefully distances us from the fable of Satan and his fallen angels, aligning it with rumor and hearsay: they were "Yearly enjoin'd, some say, to undergo / This annual" punishment (10.547–5); and the following lines emphasizing pagan tradition dispersed among the "Heathen" (10.578ff.) likewise convey the poet's skepticism about the diabolical epic (we may recall his response to the "Erring" mythology associated with Mulciber: 1.738ff.), giving it a tentative conclusion and a questionable authority. The tragic consequences of Satan's vengeful deeds will of course reverberate throughout human history (see section 19). But at this point, Milton wishes to explode the false literary tradition associated with the heroic fable of Satan and to place his hellish hate and monstrous progeny, who will ultimately be defeated by the "victorious Arm" of a truly heroic Son, in a much-needed eschatological perspective – the divine promise that "New Heav'n and Earth shall to the Ages rise / Or down from Heav'n descend" (10.634, 647–8).

11 Hell: geographical place and internal state

In *Paradise Lost*, Milton depicts Hell as both a geographical place and an internal or psychological state. As a physical place, Hell is associated with the classical underworld and with the Homeric energy we identified with Satan, as his fallen angels act with "vast *Typhoean* rage" and create a "wild uproar" (2.539, 541). Milton's Hell, furthermore, is a place characterized by its own heroic activities, worldly politics, and even grandeur. There the expatriated devils create their own community and empire: Pandemonium, which resembles an elaborate baroque structure, represents their attempt to generate a glorious civilization in their place of exile. Yet as a desolate plain and a "deep world / Of darkness" (2.262–3), this infernal world also exists at an immense distance – physically and spiritually – from Heaven: the distance of Hell to the realms of light in Heaven is three times as far as the distance from the center of the earth to the outermost sphere which envelops the earth (according to the Ptolemaic cosmological model; see 1.73–4). Milton's Hell, unlike Dante's, which extends from the surface to the center of the earth, is situated well outside this world: Milton chose not to situate Hell within the center of the earth because our world had not yet been cursed. After their defeat in Heaven in the martial epic of Book 6, the rebel angels fall for no less than nine days, suggesting the great depth of their fall, before reaching deepest Hell, "the house of woe and pain" (6.877), followed by nine days of lying vanquished and confounded there (see 1.50).

The "Dungeon horrible" (1.61) and "fiery Gulf" (1.52), with its burning lake and plain, where Satan and his legions find themselves after their Titanic fall, is a desolate, forlorn place of despair and hopelessness. It is an infernal world characterized by barrenness, mournful gloominess, and wildness; and the stunned, thunder-struck inhabitants of Milton's Hell, exiled from "the happy Realms of Light" (1.85) to a "dark opprobrious Den of shame" (2.58), are continually restless in the dismal, dreadful condition in which they now find themselves. Milton's Hell aptly recalls Dante's terrifying inscription over Hell-Gate, "All hope abandon, you who enter here" (*Inferno* III.9): the Hell of *Paradise Lost* too is a sorrowful place where "hope never comes / That comes to all" (1.66–7).

The classical elements of Milton's underworld are apparent in a particularly evocative passage like this describing

> four infernal Rivers that disgorge
> Into the burning Lake thir baleful streams;
> Abhorred *Styx* the flood of deadly hate,
> Sad *Acheron* of sorrow, black and deep;
> *Cocytus*, nam'd of lamentation loud
> Heard on the rueful stream; fierce *Phlegeton*
> Whose waves of torrent fire inflame with rage.   (2.575–81)

The personification of these four classical rivers (to be contrasted with the living streams of Heaven and the river of Paradise) itself suggests as much about the emotional and psychological nature of Milton's Hell as it does about its physical condition: the "baleful streams" recall an earlier description of Satan's "baleful eyes" (1.56) – full of evil, as well as suffering and despair as he witnesses the dismal landscape around him. The mixture of lamentation and sorrow with hatred and rage suggests that the physical place of Hell itself evokes the condition and emotional state of the devils – potentially tragic but full of Homeric fury and wrath. The landscape of Hell, moreover, is dark and wild, a place where "harpy-footed Furies" (2.596) bring the damned who suffer extremes of raging fire and frozen ice. In such an underworld the devils are tormented like thirsty Tantalus (see *Odyssey* 11.582ff.), unable to assuage their pain and sorrow by reaching the forgetful waters of Lethe, which eludes them just as waters "fled / The lip of *Tantalus*" (613–14). The myth of Tantalus, especially resonant in the poem, suggests that the restless devils are continually tantalized – their appetites are insatiable and repeatedly frustrated.

A few lines later in Book 2 Milton suggests that his Hell competes with and outdoes classical representations; here the confused devils march through

> a Region dolorous,
> O'er many a Frozen, many a Fiery Alp,
> Rocks, Caves, Lakes, Fens, Bogs, Dens, and shades of death,
> A Universe of death, which God by curse
> Created evil, for evil only good,
> Where all life dies, death lives, and Nature breeds,
> Perverse, all monstrous, all prodigious things,
> Abominable, inutterable, and worse
> Than Fables yet have feign'd, or fear conceiv'd,
> *Gorgons* and *Hydras*, and *Chimeras* dire.   (619–28)

Such a dreary, barren landscape underscores the ambiguous nature of Milton's Hell, hardly a universe at all and a place of spiritual death: it is a parody of Heaven and of the providential order where God creates good out of evil. Its wasteland exists in sharp contrast to the sensuous fertility of Milton's Eden. Line 621, in which each word is a monosyllable, suggests that this dead landscape consists of a series of nearly intractable objects. This is a world which Milton also characterizes by paradox and oxymoron – "death lives" or "darkness visible" (1.63; recalling Job 10:22: "A land of darkness . . . where the light is as darkness"). The perverse and monstrous things of the poem's underworld are certainly classical in nature – Gorgons,

Hydras, Chimeras – but they also outdo earlier imaginative representations since here, Milton tells us, they are "Worse / Than Fables yet have feign'd." Even in his representation of Hell, then, Milton rivals again his epic precursors, creating a world that is more horrifying than anything their poetic fictions have represented.

Yet however dreary this infernal landscape may be, the devils give their underworld existence a dynamic quality as they manage to channel their Homeric energy into various physical, artistic, and intellectual activities. We see them as Homeric-style soldiers: music in Hell encourages their heroic firmness and discipline, just as it "rais'd / To highth of noblest temper Heroes old / Arming to Battle" (1.551–3). Some devils engage in activities that remind us of a Greek city-state, including epic games and mimic battles (2.528ff.); such epic activities evoke an older heroic world like that of the *Iliad* or the *Aeneid*, Book 5. Other devils turn out to be epic poets singing of their own self-glorification (2.546ff.), the very subject of Satanic epic, as they suspend Hell with their ravishing song. Meanwhile, others engage in philosophical discourse, debating theological issues central to Milton's poem, including questions debated in the heavenly council of Book 3; these devils reason

> Of Providence, Foreknowledge, Will, and Fate,
> Fixt Fate, Free will, Foreknowledge absolute.   (2.559–60)

Lost in "wand'ring mazes," a labyrinth of error, the devils find "no end" (2.561) to their discourse and reasoning since that end, of course, resides in God.

The dynamic world of Milton's Hell is likewise characterized as a place of empire, politics, and government. In their exile, the rebel angels heroically build their own civilization, much as mankind in exile will do after the Fall, as Adam learns from Michael's prophecy in Books 11 and 12. The devils' most magnificent creation – admired even by the poet himself – is the baroque palace and capital of Pandemonium, Satan's city and "proud seat" (10.424), which outdoes the greatest of all earthly monuments and pagan cities:

> Not *Babylon*,
> Nor great *Alcairo* such magnificence
> Equall'd in all thir glories . . .   (1.717–19)

The impression of Milton's description of the richly adorned Pandemonium – with its roof of "fretted Gold," its "Doric pillars overlaid / With Golden Architrave" and including cornices and friezes with projecting sculptures – is far from simply negative in its effect. The reader may indeed admire its splendor (recalling buildings Milton saw on his Italian journey), as well as the industry and energy of the restless devils to create something magnificent out of their desolate, forlorn environment. The details of Milton's description of this "wondrous Art" (1.703) in Hell, then, provoke in the reader a more complicated response to the creative and social energy of the exiled devils, only recently God's angels and members of the heavenly order.

The infernal council of Satan and his grand peers, which takes place within Pandemonium, especially focuses our attention on Hell as a realm of worldly activities, politics, and demagoguery. The magnificent titles of these devils who appear in the "infernal Court" (1.792) highlight their august political stature: they are called "great Seraphic Lords" (1.794), "Powers and Dominions" (2.11), "Synod of Gods" (2.391); the fierce and despairing Moloch is called "Scepter'd King" (2.43). Here we see them, like active and scheming politicians, debating future actions that will affect their empire and diminished power, as well as the precarious future of mankind. The devils air their different, even clashing viewpoints: Moloch in favor of immediate war, Belial in favor of doing nothing, Mammon in favor of empire building in Hell, Beelzebub in favor of conquering God's new race of man. Their competing and conflicting arguments suggest that Milton's Hell is an intensely political world where different counsels and policies are formulated, debated, dismissed or recommended. With a fine ear for political rhetoric and posturing – his rebel angels are brilliant orators – Milton has made the devilish assembly in Hell come alive for the reader of his poem.

Thus far we have been considering Milton's Hell as an infernal place of punishment and exile; and we have noted the social, political, and creative activities which occur in this gloomy place, making the devils' fallen civilization a dynamic underworld. But Hell – Satan's realm – is not only a physical or geographical place located at a vast distance from earth and Heaven: in *Paradise Lost*, as we began to see in the previous section, it is no less significantly a subjective, psychological, and interior state. In that sense, it is a place with no physical limits at all. The internalization of Hell was a powerful notion in the late Renaissance, as the sobering words of Marlowe's Mephistophilis make clear when he responds to Doctor Faustus's inquiry concerning "the place that men call hell":

> Hell hath no limits nor is circumscribed
> In one self place. But where we are is hell,
> And where hell is there must we ever be.
>
> > (*Doctor Faustus*, 1.5.119, 124–6; *The Complete Plays*,
> > ed. J. B. Steane [1969])

Or as Sir Thomas Browne observed in his *Religio Medici* (1643), in response to the popular preoccupation with Hell as a place of physical torments and "flaming mountaines" or volcanoes: "I feele sometimes a hell within my selfe, *Lucifer* keeps his court in my breast" (1.51). To be sure, the geographical Hell of *Paradise Lost* has its fiery lake and its volcano belching flames and smoke. But Milton's poem also dramatizes the notion that Hell exists within and where Satan is: the chiasmus in the narrator's lines – "The Hell within him, for within him Hell / He brings" (4.20–1) – underscores rhetorically Hell as an inner state. With his tormented and restless mind, Satan carries Hell within him wherever he goes – no matter how far that may be from the physical place of Hell. Even when he gazes, as voyeur, on the happier Eden of Adam and Eve, Satan finds that he cannot escape from that Hell where he is "thrust" (4.508).

Indeed, the notion of Hell as an internal, psychological, and spiritual state applies not only to Satan, but also to the inner torment of Adam and Eve after the Fall: thus "Thir inward State of Mind" (9.1125ff.) becomes turbulent, restless, and full of discord; and the despairing Adam in Book 10 feels that he has fallen into a terrible "Abyss of fears / And horrors" (10.842–3), much like the dramatic Satan who fears "a lower deep" as he suffers from his internal state of Hell (4.75ff.). For Milton, then, an internal Hell is no less real and no less powerful a concept than its external, physical manifestations. If paradise lies within – an interior and symbolic state as the end of this Protestant poem teaches its readers – then so does Hell itself.

12 God, providence, and free will

Paradise Lost highlights the dramatic contrast between the realms of darkness and light by moving from Hell and its infernal council, in Books 1 and 2, to Heaven in Book 3, where the celestial colloquy between God and the Son (lines 56–343) takes place concerning the poem's central theological themes, including the crucial issue of human free will. Yet Milton's bold depiction of God the Father here and elsewhere in the epic has often unsettled or antagonized readers of the poem. Alexander Pope called him "a School-Divine" and in the twentieth century William Empson even went so far as to suggest that Milton's picture of God in the poem "is astonishingly like Uncle Joe Stalin" (*Milton's God*, p. 146). Empson's modern comparison may seem perverse; yet readers may indeed find themselves disturbed by the harshness of the divine decree, as well as its legal formulation, when God, addressing his Son, calls man an "ingrate" (3.97) or insists that disobedient man

> with his whole posterity must die,
> Die hee or Justice must; unless for him
> Some other able, and as willing, pay
> The rigid satisfaction, death for death.   (3.209–12)

Of course, in attempting to represent God in his epic poem, Milton was taking a great artistic chance: might he not, in Marvell's words, "ruin . . . The sacred Truths to Fable"? How, after all, does the bold Protestant poet present the omnipotent deity – "Author of all being" (3.374) – to his readers in a poem that appears to valorize human free will and agency? In Book 3 of *Paradise Lost* Milton does it dramatically and artistically, and it is here especially that we can begin to appreciate the literary and theological daring of his depiction of the Godhead.

The council in Heaven in Book 3, an imaginative revision of the celestial council scene found in classical epics, enables Milton to present, as he puts it in his *Christian Doctrine*, "that play-acting of the persons of the godhead" (YP 6:213). Indeed, already in one of the early drafts of the poem, contained in the Trinity College Manuscript, Milton had conceived of a debate in Heaven between Justice, Mercy, and Wisdom on "what should become of man if he fall" as part of the first act of a dramatic work entitled "Paradise Lost" (YP 8:554). And so in the epic *Paradise Lost* both Father and Son appear as dramatic characters as they address, in their dialogue, such central theological issues as divine justice, free will, sufficient grace, determinism, and providential foreknowledge. While God's speeches in the heavenly scene highlight the freedom of choice – a theme central to the poem as we have seen – their sternness in regard to fallen humankind (the Fall, of course, has yet to occur) is nevertheless often sharp and unsettling. To be sure, this turns out to be an emotionally charged section of the poem – for the reader as well as for God. Knowing that man will transgress the "Sole pledge of his obedience" (3.95) and, unlike the loyal angels during the great war in Heaven, fail to stand firm (see section 16), God seems accusatory and speaks defensively as he righteously justifies his own ways to his Son:

> whose fault?
> Whose but his own? ingrate, he had of mee
> All he could have; I made him just and right,
> Sufficient to have stood, though free to fall.   (3.96–9)

Yet having recently been betrayed by the faithless Satan and his rebel angels, who themselves had the power of choice and free will ("Freely they stood who stood, and fell who fell," 3.102), God is clearly anxious about being betrayed again – and this time by man himself, his newest creation. The Father's response, then, is hardly a disengaged justification of his doctrinal decrees and demands. To the contrary, God speaks here like an angry, irritable, and passionate parent concerned about his "youngest Son" (3.151); and while God intends to show mankind mercy (lines 132–4, 202), from which none is excluded, he also feels compelled to show justice. Indeed, the angelic song following the dialogue between Father and Son refers to the Son appeasing the conflict within God himself: "Hee to appease thy wrath, and end the strife / Of Mercy and Justice in thy face discern'd" (3.406–7). In these remarkable lines, as elsewhere in Book 3's heavenly council, Milton dares to portray a God of emotions himself struggling with his own decrees and with the poem's central theological issues. In the process, Milton's God feels not only such emotions as wrath and indignation, but also "pity" (3.405).

Milton's belief in the exercise of human free will in order to achieve salvation, we saw in section 5, is essentially a radical form of Arminianism and a rejection of the stark Calvinist determinism that prevailed in early seventeenth-century orthodox Protestant theology and that was common among Calvinist Puritans. God may have foreknowledge in *Paradise Lost*, but he has in no sense predetermined the fall of mankind – man falls freely and possesses the means to resist temptation. The issue of freedom thus enables Milton's theodicy to exonerate God from the responsibility for the Fall. God himself reiterates this point after the Fall, when he reminds the angels and the Son that "no Decree of mine" was "Concurring to necessitate his Fall, / Or touch with lightest moment of impulse / His free will" (10.44–6). Justifying his ways during the heavenly council, God stresses the poem's Arminian emphasis on man's free agency in his salvation:

> So without least impulse or shadow of Fate,
> Or aught by me immutably foreseen,
> They trespass, Authors to themselves in all
> Both what they judge and what they choose; for so
> I form'd them free, and free they must remain,
> Till they enthrall themselves.   (3.120–5)

God's decrees do not work by "shadow of Fate" or immutable destiny, as though *Paradise Lost* were a pagan epic like the *Aeneid*, which associates the will of Jupiter with the expression of Fate. Indeed, the providential cosmos of *Paradise Lost*, with its emphasis on God's sovereignty, discounts any notion of a capricious Fortune, Fate or Chance familiar from classical times and the Middle Ages. (Only the devils believe that God's supremacy is upheld in terms of a pagan trinity of "strength, or Chance, or Fate" [1.133].) Moreover, quite unlike any traditional Calvinist writer, Milton imagines in his poem a dynamic prelapsarian world in which human beings "by degrees of merit rais'd" may work their way up to Heaven (7.157–61) since they, as God observes, are "Authors to themselves" in "what they judge and what they choose." For these reasons, the angel Raphael explains to Adam that his will – "By nature free" – is in no way ruled "by Fate / Inextricable, or strict necessity" (5.527–8). In fact, when it comes to obeying or disobeying, Milton's angels themselves are

no less free to choose, as even Satan himself admits in his first soliloquy: "Hadst thou the same free Will and Power to stand? / Thou
hadst" (4.66–7). The freedom of choice in determining one's spiritual destiny is, of course, central to Milton's poetics of temptation
in *Paradise Lost*: by stressing that "Man shall find grace" (3.131)
after falling (unlike the rebel angels), God further underscores the
poem's Arminian theology, which sets *Paradise Lost* apart from the
more orthodox Calvinist determinism of Milton's age.

Milton, then, has given his radical Protestant poem a serious
and daring theological dimension, which he has chosen to develop
dramatically and poetically rather than to present as pure, untested
doctrine. Nevertheless, the poem's concern with God's omnipotence
(e.g. 3.372ff.) and his omniscience (his vision of "past, present, future," 3.78), on the one hand, and its emphasis on human freedom
and responsibility, on the other, does create a tension that is by no
means fully resolved in *Paradise Lost*. Clearly Milton valued human
freedom and voluntary choice and made them central to his greatest poem; and yet he still will not give up the idea of God's absolute
power. This tension contributes to the unsettling effect of the drama
of Heaven in Book 3 and to the unease so often registered by readers.
Of course, while Milton's God is all-powerful and all-seeing, he is not
simply a God of arbitrary will, but, significantly, a God of "permis-
sive will" (3.685) who "Hinder'd not *Satan* to attempt the mind /
Of Man" (10.8–9), thus allowing both Satan and humankind to exercise their freedom of unconstrained choice. Still, whether or not
one decides that Milton is fully successful in his depiction of God the
Father, one needs at least to recognize how daring Milton is to explore
theological doctrine in this way – that is, to dramatize the persons
of his heterodox Godhead themselves actively debating and struggling with the poem's central theological notions. Although often
unsettling and fraught with tension, this dramatic and emotional
presentation enables the poet to accommodate the transcendent
Godhead to the fallen reader.

The Son of God himself, the embodiment of mercy, divine love,
and voluntary obedience, emerges as a distinctive and challenging
voice in this dramatic and highly charged section of the poem, so
much so that he dares to question the Almighty Father on crucial theological matters. The Son, we saw in section 5, is conceived

by Milton as an independent being, distinct in essence from the
"Omnipotent / Eternal Father" (7.136–7; cf. 8.406–8) and subordinate to him; the first of all created things, the Son is begotten in time
not from eternity (3.384; 5.603; 7.163) and he does not share his
Father's omniscience. Milton the radical Protestant does not hide
his heresies: he diverges from orthodox Trinitarianism both in his
theological conception of the Son (as in the *Christian Doctrine*) and
in his poetic dramatization of him. What Milton presents in *Paradise
Lost*, then, is a dynamic Son who demonstrates, in the process of
active debate and dialogue, that he is indeed "By Merit more than
Birthright Son of God" (3.309). Even in terms of heaven's hierarchy,
Milton imagines a meritocracy of virtue radically different from an
older-style aristocratic hierarchy based on birth: this is a Son who
proves his merit and right to power by choosing freely to serve and
obey God's will.

In Book 3 the Son at first joins in eloquently praising God for making grace available to man (144ff.) – a means of salvation which,
from the poem's Arminian perspective, man has the freedom to accept or reject. But then the Son immediately launches into a series
of challenging questions and observations (150–64), as though he
himself is testing God's divine decrees, eternal purpose, and judgement on mankind: shall Satan "fulfil / His malice, and thy goodness
bring to naught," the Son dares to ask the Almighty; "or wilt thou
thyself / Abolish thy Creation, and unmake, / For him, what for thy
glory thou hast made?" And so while "the Father is greater than the
Son in all things" (YP 6:223), as Milton observes in his theological
tract, the relation between Father and Son in *Paradise Lost* is hardly
static, as this highly dramatic passage and subsequent ones suggest.
Rather, Milton presents their crucial exchange in the celestial council as dynamic and dialectic: the Son, like the recently-born Adam
in Book 8, boldly exercises his freedom to debate with the Almighty,
even to the point of daring to suggest that, should Satan's revenge
and hellish hate succeed, God's vulnerable goodness and greatness
might "Be question'd and blasphem'd without defense" (3.166).
God's subsequent response (3.168ff.) does indeed assure the Son
that man will be saved, thanks to heavenly grace "Freely voutsaf't,"
although even here the Father's speech can become defensive and

stern: frail fallen man, God insists, owes "to me" "All his deliv'rance, and to none but me."

The heavenly drama seems no less tense when God raises the crucial issue of sacrifice and redemption for humankind (3.210ff.). Pronouncing the tough demands and logic of divine justice, the Father himself appears harsh and legalistic, asking which of the heavenly powers will "pay / The rigid satisfaction, death for death." Indeed, the unsettling response God receives at first is nothing less than an awesome silence: "all the Heav'nly Choir stood mute" (3.217), as though no power were willing to make the great sacrifice on behalf of fallen humankind. This tense moment of uncertainty is meant to recall the mute response of the devils in reaction to Beelzebub's call for a daring savior and destroyer among their fallen legions. The Son's subsequent and willing offer of himself as sacrifice – "Behold mee then, mee for him, life for life / I offer, on mee let thine anger fall" (3.236ff.) – not only parallels Satan's offer in Book 2, as well as Eve's sacrifice in Book 10; it is also that dramatic moment which most fully proves the Son's merit. Both engaged and actively tested by the dramatic exchange in Heaven, the Son is found true. Moreover, unlike heroic Satan who seeks deliverance for his exiled nation, even as he aims to destroy God's new race, the heroic Son will save nothing less than the entire creation. His offer thus transforms the very notion of epic action and makes possible the divine salvation and restoration which the second half of Milton's poem elaborates: "So Heav'nly love shall outdo Hellish hate" (3.298). Freely chosen obedience in *Paradise Lost*, manifested perfectly by the self-sacrificing Son in this scene, is a sign of strength made perfect in weakness – that favorite Miltonic theme. The angelic praise the Son receives in Heaven for his voluntary offer significantly merges with the inspired praise of the visionary poet himself: "Hail Son of God, Savior of Men, thy Name / Shall be the copious matter of my Song" (3.412–13).

The celestial colloquy in Book 3, then, enables Milton to dramatize controversial doctrinal issues which are important not only to Protestantism but to Milton's own passionate belief in the individual free will of all God's divine and human sons. If the reader finds these dramatic heavenly exchanges unsettling at a number of key points, that is precisely because Milton has also made the central theological issues of his poem deeply challenging. Milton's dramatic poem intensely engages the reader, prompting him or her to question, actively think about, and – even like the Father and Son themselves – to debate and struggle with its major theological themes. And so with *Paradise Lost*, the epic has become a poetic medium for imaginatively representing controversial but crucial theological issues. In his influential work of Renaissance literary criticism, *Discourses on the Heroic Poem* (1594) – a work that Milton himself knew well – Torquatto Tasso had suggested that a poet "is not to show himself ambitious in . . . theological questions" (trans. M. Cavalchini and I. Samuel [1973], p. 51), leaving such matters to schools of theologians. But clearly for John Milton, the heroic English poet who has chosen a Biblical subject for his visionary epic, ambitious theological questions are absolutely central to his great poetic enterprise. Writing as both artist and theologian, the radical Protestant poet revitalizes controversial doctrinal themes, treating them in his Biblical epic with unusual power and drama – as he does so notably in the celestial colloquy of Book 3.

13 Milton's Eden

Paradise Lost shifts from the divine to the human in Book 4, where it begins to give the reader a full and splendid depiction of Eden. In Milton's sacred poem, the Fall is unfortunate partly because unfallen Paradise, presented from Books 4 to 8, offers such a sensuous and pleasurable way of life for Adam and Eve. But life in Eden, which means "delight" or "place of pleasure," is far from languorous or idle. Rather this earthly Paradise, for all its sensuous and pastoral delights, is a complex environment where Adam and Eve find themselves continually challenged and where life is always dynamic and characterized by "ceaseless change" (5.183). Milton's poem describes Edenic life with great care and artfulness, making us value the rich pleasures of this vital but vulnerable Paradise from which our first parents were sadly exiled.

Milton's luxuriant Paradise, the garden located within the land of Eden (see 4.209ff.), recalls and revises a whole European tradition of gardens and mythic paradises, including Dante's Paradise on the top of Mount Purgatory, Spenser's Garden of Adonis, Sidney's

Arcadia, as well as numerous classical and Biblical incarnations. Indeed, as Milton makes clear, his pleasurable and sacred Eden surpasses all other classical and literary versions when he provides a negative catalogue of gardens ("Not that fair field / Of *Enna* . . . nor that sweet Grove / of *Daphne* . . .") which cannot compare "with this Paradise / Of *Eden*" (4.268–81; cf. 9.439–43). This fertile Paradise is everywhere characterized by its sensuous richness and particularity: the poet describes the rich trees laden with "fairest Fruit, / Blossoms and Fruits at once of golden hue / Appear'd, with gay enamell'd colors mixt" (4.147–9) – a passage suggesting the fusion of artfulness and nature in Eden. The river of Paradise, rising as a "Sapphire Fount" and its brooks rolling over "Orient Pearl and sands of Gold," is likewise described in aureate diction suggesting ornateness (4.237–8). And the nuptial bower of Adam and Eve is itself described in terms of aesthetic details which convey its intricate natural art: thus "the sovran Planter" "fram'd / All things to man's delightful use" and "Broider'd the ground" with violet, crocus, and hyacinth, a "rich inlay" "more color'd than with stone / Of costliest Emblem" (4.690ff.). With its sweet odors, artful landscape, and delicious and various fruits, Milton's "profuse" (4.243) Paradise, containing "Nature's whole wealth" (4.207), fully satisfies sight, smell, and taste. Furthermore, it possesses an abundance and fecundity that tends towards excess and wanton growth: "A Wilderness of sweets; for Nature here / Wanton'd in her prime . . . pouring forth more sweet, / Wild above Rule or Art, enormous bliss" (5.294–7).

As "A happy rural seat of various view" (4.247), Milton's Eden is, moreover, a pastoral landscape. The younger Virgilian-style poet of *Lycidas* may have moved on to "fresh Woods, and Pastures new" by attempting more ambitious genres like epic (see section 2), but rather than altogether abandoning the pastoral mode, he has imaginatively reincorporated it into *Paradise Lost*. Between the fair trees of Eden

> Lawns, or level Downs, and Flocks
> Grazing the tender herb, were interpos'd,
> Or palmy hillock, or the flow'ry lap
> Of some irriguous Valley spread her store,
> Flow'rs of all hue . . .   (4.252–6)

The conjunction "or" suggests the alternatives available to the reader of Milton's epic, encouraged here to imagine the rich variety of this original pastoral world of innocence – one, as we shall see, by no means associated with a simple, childlike, or rustic life.

Despite the wondrous pleasures and pastoral elements of Edenic life, our first parents remain fully active in their paradisal existence. In the morning and evening they engage in inspired hymns and "holy rapture" as they praise their maker (as we see in Books 4 and 5); and they also need to work, beginning early in the day, pruning the growing plants and tending the flowers, herbs, and fruits. As a place of vital change, growth, as well as considerable wildness and excess, Eden indeed needs to be looked after and cultivated. Other creatures may roam idly, but not Adam and Eve, who engage in a process of creative horticultural reform as they attempt to maintain order in Eden. Their life in Paradise is thus both pastoral and georgic: as gardeners rather than shepherds or herdsmen (the more common occupations of Arcadian or Golden Age pastoral), they "reform / Yon flow'ry Arbors, yonder Alleys green . . . with branches overgrown" (4.625–7). This active work life in Eden is further complemented by plenty of intellectual discussion and challenge. With the appearance in Book 5 of their divine instructor, the archangel Raphael (see section 15), their varied and complex Edenic life assumes a more intellectual and philosophical dimension (though never at the expense of the sensuous).

Nor is this rich, sensuous life in prelapsarian Eden free from crisis or tension. Indeed, in Book 4 we are often keenly aware of Satan's threatening perspective and presence in the garden. Despite the garden's natural protections, including a wilderness of "Insuperable highth" and walls of trees, the furtive and voyeuristic Satan easily gets into it (see 4.135ff. and 179ff.): he is compared to a wolf invading God's sheepfold (only one of many shapes he is associated with in the poem), reminding us how vulnerable and fragile this delightful place or *locus amoenus* is as we begin to share his view of its beauty and abundant pleasures (4.205ff.). Well before the Fall, Satan also invades the secret nuptial bower of Adam and Eve (see 4.797ff.): there he tries to corrupt the imagination of the sleeping Eve by using his "Devilish art" to create a demonic dream. The fiend is immediately discovered by angelic guards, prompting him to flee from Eden (he will return in Book 9, after circling the earth for seven days); nevertheless, his first temptation of Eve, which prefigures the temptation and Fall of Book 9, reminds us of the close and precarious proximity of good and evil in Milton's Paradise. The experience of the dream – including Satan's amorous and "gentle voice" and the angel-like figure enticing Eve to taste the fruit (see 5.28ff.) – deeply unsettles Eve, while affecting Adam "equally" (5.97); the crisis does, moreover, heighten our parents' unusual intimacy, which is not in Genesis itself (5.129ff.). Even in unfallen Paradise, then, Adam and Eve find themselves faced with and tested by a troubling crisis which they manage to work through together. It is fitting that, immediately after this first critical experience in Eden, they should hasten to the light and field to offer their prayers and begin their morning's active work in the garden.

14 Adam and Eve and human sexuality

When Milton focuses our attention in Book 4 on the paradisal life of first man and woman, he makes human sexuality and passion central to his great epic. Indeed, from Book 4 to Book 9, Milton's poem explores the prelapsarian relation between the sexes and represents the full richness of human sexuality and wedded love. *Paradise Lost* valorizes the life of the senses, human eroticism and passion: all are essential to Milton's paradisal ideal. Yet his poem's representation of sexual hierarchy has sometimes troubled modern readers: is its depiction of the sexes patriarchal or egalitarian? Critics have sometimes considered Milton among the great patriarchal poets in English literature, and there are certainly passages in the poem which seem patriarchal in emphasis. Nevertheless, this intensely passionate and sensuous poem cannot be categorized so easily, for it often vacillates between patriarchal and egalitarian models of sexual relations. When it comes to representing the complex relations between the sexes, *Paradise Lost* is often equivocal and even contradictory about the issue of hierarchy versus equality.

Let us look at one of the most famous passages in Book 4, a sensuous description which already begins to register the tension between sexual equality and hierarchy in *Paradise Lost*. The poem's first depiction of our happy mother and father in their unfallen

paradise highlights their nobility, dignity, and perfection, their unfallen aristocratic posture as they rule over the sacred garden of
Eden. Here they appear "Godlike erect, with native Honor clad /
In naked Majesty seem'd Lords of all" (4.289–90). In this state of
innocence, Adam and Eve are paradoxically adorned by their very
nakedness, and their "naked Majesty" is not at all like the earthly
majesty of European kings and queens. But then the passage begins
to distinguish between the sexes:

> though both
> Not equal, as thir sex not equal seem'd;
> For contemplation hee and valor form'd,
> For softness shee and sweet attractive Grace,
> Hee for God only, shee for God in him.   (4.295–9)

Such lines, with the negative construction "not equal seem'd," suggest a patriarchal view of gender relations: the last line especially
is Pauline in its suggestion that the man is the head of the woman
and that the wife should submit herself to the husband (as in Eph-
esians 5:22). Genesis itself, it is worth recalling, says nothing about
the submission of woman to man until after the Fall (see 3:16). Of
course, our response to Milton's lines is complicated by the fact that
the voyeuristic Satan is the one enviously gazing upon the primal
couple and their Edenic delights (4.285–7, 356), a detail emphasized by the verb "seem'd." This makes it more difficult to assume
that throughout the passage we are simply getting the narrator's
own perspective. The passage also suggests that Adam and Eve do
possess different qualities and virtues. Still, it is not quite accurate
to conclude from these lines that Milton's intelligent Eve is unable
to comprehend abstruse intellectual matters: as Milton suggests in
Book 8, Eve is interested in Raphael's educational discourse ("Of
what was high"), but prefers to hear about it from her husband,
who makes intellectual conversation a more pleasurable, erotic
experience by "solv[ing] high dispute / With conjugal Caresses"
(48–57).

Even as it conveys a sense of sexual hierarchy and difference,
Milton's elaborate description of first woman draws upon a luxurious and amorous vocabulary that, in the context of Eden's valorized
eroticism, enhances rather than diminishes Eve's powers:

Shee as a veil down to the slender waist
Her unadorned golden tresses wore
Dishevell'd, but in wanton ringlets wav'd
As the Vine curls her tendrils, which impli'd
Subjection, but requir'd with gentle sway,
And by her yielded, by him best receiv'd,
Yielded with coy submission, modest pride,
And sweet reluctant amorous delay.   (4.304–11)

This rich passage evokes the eroticism of Eve's dishevelled and loose hair – "a veil" that hides and reveals simultaneously: "Nor those mysterious parts were then conceal'd / Then was not guilty shame" (312–13), the poet adds a few lines later. He thus emphasizes the purity of Edenic sexuality free from those "shows" (316) which have troubled postlapsarian mankind. Words like "Dishevell'd" and "wanton" convey a sensuous yet unfallen resonance in this particular context, while the phrase "Sweet reluctant amorous delay" captures perfectly the sensuousness of sexual foreplay in Milton's Paradise. The erotic language associated with Adam and Eve – their "youthful dalliance" and her "attractive Grace" (4.338, 298) – redeems such language previously associated with Sin and Satan (2.762, 819).

As we saw in section 3, Milton's *Areopagitica* stressed that God created "passions within us, pleasures round about us" and "these rightly temper'd are the very ingredients of vertu" (YP 2:527). As a poem about the pleasures of wedded love, *Paradise Lost* explicitly valorizes human passion and sexuality in such a way as to suggest equality in the erotic partnership. James Grantham Turner has recently called the poem "an erotology" (*One Flesh*, p. 232) and there are plenty of passages to support that description. One of the most famous occurs later in Book 4 (lines 736–75); there, Milton describes the intimate act of lovemaking which takes place in the "inmost bower" of Adam and Eve at night, as if to crown the achievements of their working day. The poet stresses the intense mutuality of Adam and Eve's sexual relationship, free of "These troublesome disguises which wee wear": their reciprocity is underscored as Milton describes how they lay down "side by side" and chose to make love ("nor turn'd I ween / *Adam* from his fair Spouse, nor *Eve* the Rites / Mysterious of connubial Love refus'd"). Only "Hypocrites," the poet insists, would deny the purity, innocence, and satisfaction of their sexual intercourse. The one figure in the poem who would bid them "abstain" from conjugal love – the tormented, sneering Satan – is himself sexually frustrated and "with pain of longing pines" (4.511) as he jealously observes the sweet nuptial embraces and kissing between Adam and Eve (see 492ff.). In his hymn to wedded love of Book 4, the unabashed poet of paradisal eroticism has come a long way from the emotionally troubled divorce tracts he had written in the 1640s (after Mary Powell, his first wife, had left him), where he suggested that "the carnal act . . . might seem to have something of pollution in it" – even in the state of innocence (*Doctrine and Discipline*, YP 2:326).

Indeed, in *Paradise Lost* Milton presents sexual love in marriage as holy and beautiful, and worthy of "mysterious reverence" (8.599), as Adam himself will explain to his first angelic tutor. Associated with fruitful progeny (4.732–4), it manifests the fertility of creation and of Paradise itself:

> Hail wedded Love, mysterious Law, true source
> Of human offspring, sole propriety
> In Paradise of all things in common else.
> By thee adulterous lust was driv'n from men
> Among the bestial herds to range . . .   (750–4)

Later the angel Raphael, discussing human passion and sexuality with a rapturous Adam, will compare human sexual love to "carnal pleasure" and animal copulation: "think the same voutsaf't / To Cattle and each Beast" (8.593, 581–2); and yet Adam is only "half abash't" (8.595) by this interpretation of human lovemaking. Adam then proceeds to defend human love and passion (8.596ff.), claiming that they are really more complex (they involve "Union of Mind" and "Soul" [604]) than his divine instructor has suggested. The poet of *Paradise Lost* would seem to agree with Adam: the sexual love he celebrates in the "Hail wedded love" passage of Book 4 is not bestial copulation but something higher, something more refined and purer.

The challenge Milton faces as a fallen poet is how to write about such intimate lovemaking and mutuality in Eden: "Far be it, that I should write thee sin or blame, / Or think thee unbefitting holiest place" (4.758–9). Milton draws on the literary language of secular love poetry ("Here Love his golden shafts imploys" [763]) only to purify it in this sacred context of praising Edenic sexuality; moreover, the negative catalogue which follows (4.765ff.) disassociates the poet's erotic subject and writing from its more tainted Renaissance and Cavalier manifestations, where love and revelling are often associated with "Court Amours, / Mixt Dance, or wanton Mask." In contrast to the sexually fulfilled Adam and Eve is "the starv'd Lover" of the popular Petrarchan literary tradition who is "quitted with disdain" by his "proud" mistress. Significantly, Satan later begins his temptation of Eve with the lavish rhetoric of Petrarchan love poetry (9.532ff.). Such contemporary love poetry, in addition to the Cavalier society Milton associates with it, prevents or debases the natural sexual intimacy which Milton's poem unabashedly celebrates. Nothing indeed, except perhaps lovemaking in Heaven (see 8.618ff.), could surpass the delights of Edenic sexuality, as the poet's concluding lines to this passage remind us: "Sleep on, / Blest pair; and O yet happiest if ye seek / No happier state, and know to know no more" (4.773–5). His comment on the sleeping postcoital couple, registering that uneasy tension between his (and our) fallen perspective and Adam and Eve's unfallen state, reminds us once more that the Fall was by no means fortunate.

In offering a rich exploration of human sexuality and passion, *Paradise Lost* is too complex to conform to a consistent or unified model of sexual relations. To be sure, the poem does at times configure the relation between the sexes in patriarchal terms, as we began to see earlier in this section. Thus just after her autobiographical account of passing narcissism (where we learn that she turns from admiring her own watery image to admiring the more substantial Adam), the narrator describes Eve's "meek surrender" and Adam smiling "with superior Love" as our primal father takes great delight in Eve's erotic "Beauty and submissive Charms" (494–9): it is hard to escape the supremacist implications of this description, though when Adam himself openly discusses his passion with Raphael, he denies feeling superior (8.546ff.). Indeed, the more carefully we read *Paradise Lost*, the more we notice the poem's conflicting impulses.

Consider, for example, Eve's remarkable love song in Book 4. Just before her song she addresses Adam in a series of Pauline clichés,

appealing to masculine authority by calling him "Author and Disposer" and then observing:

> what thou bidd'st
> Unargu'd I obey; so God ordains,
> God is thy Law, thou mine; to know no more
> Is woman's happiest knowledge and her praise.   (635–8)

Such self-abnegating lines conform perfectly well to St. Paul's message about the man being the head of the woman (see 1 Cor. 11:3).
But Eve's stunning lines which immediately follow (639ff.) – a fine
instance of prelapsarian lyricism – undermine these Pauline plati-
tudes. Speaking of her subjective sense of time with Adam ("With
thee conversing I forget all time"), she now reveals herself to be an
exquisite love poet. Her sensuous, lyrical voice is underscored by the
sibilants of her poetry as she describes the fragrance of "the fertile
earth / After soft showers; and sweet the coming on / Of grateful
Ev'ning mild, then silent Night / With this her solemn Bird . . ." Yet
only with Adam are all these delightful, natural moments "sweet,"
the word which begins and ends her sixteen-line love song (641–56),
finely illustrating poetic epanalepsis (Greek for "a taking up again").
Eve is in fact the first love poet in Paradise and her performance, with
its own distinctive, highly amorous poetic voice, clearly qualifies the
dutiful notion that Adam is her "Author" (which of course he is
not). Here is one place, then, where we can see her own rich poetry undermining the Pauline model of masculine authority. Her
sensuous, passionate poetry, moreover, aligns her creative powers
with the poetics of Milton himself, who believed that poetry should
be "simple, sensuous and passionate" (*Of Education*, YP 2:403). Indeed, the "solemn Bird" Eve sings about – the amorous nightingale
associated with her nuptial bower – is itself an emblem of Milton's
own artistic powers (3.38–40) in a poem inspired by a female Muse,
the "Celestial Patroness" (9.21).

A particularly striking example of the way the poem challenges
conventional patriarchal notions of subordination occurs in Book 8,
in the lively colloquy between Adam and God. This is the passage in
which Adam, just recently born and already restless in his solitude,
asks God for a helpmate (8.364–451). In Genesis, we should recall,
it is God who notices that Adam is alone: "It is not good that the man

should be alone; I will make him an help meet for him" (2:18). But in Milton's revision of this Biblical text, it is Adam himself who discovers this basic ontological need – the need for another, and in this case that other, Adam observes, is nothing less than an equal partner: "Among unequals what society / Can sort, what harmony or true delight?" Both "presumptuous" and respectful towards the Father in this scene, Adam speaks with great emotional conviction of the mutuality upon which this fellowship must be based: "but in disparity / The one intense, the other still remiss / Cannot well suit with either, but soon prove / Tedious alike." Adam's musical metaphor of strings, which need to be tuned to the same intensity, conveys the conviction of his observation. God at first responds to Adam, however, by saying that he himself lives "solitary," like a bachelor, and so why in effect shouldn't Adam: "for none I know / Second to mee or like, equal much less." Here again Adam answers the Almighty like a respectful but feisty pupil, distinguishing between man's needs and God's; God is perfect in himself, but Adam genuinely desires and needs "Collateral love, and dearest amity," as well as "Social communication." Marriage, Adam instinctively perceives, exists to cure the "defects" of solitude. (In his divorce tracts, Milton notes "the lonelines which leads [man] still powerfully to seek a fit help," YP 2:253.) Indeed, nothing at all is said in this spirited exchange between Adam and God about the subordination of woman to man. And rather than rebuking Adam for presumptuously requesting an equal, God is clearly pleased by his new son's bold responses and lively intelligence: the Almighty is playfully testing his youngest son – for God often challenges his creatures in *Paradise Lost* – and Adam in turn uses his "freedom" to argue with the Almighty. This spirited colloquy concludes, moreover, with God promising to give Adam precisely the "equal" consort he so passionately desires: "What next I bring shall please thee, be assur'd, / Thy likeness, thy fit help, thy other self, / Thy wish, exactly to thy heart's desire." Milton's poem, then, can respond with great inventiveness and emotional conviction to the ideal of egalitarian love.

But then how do we reconcile the discussion between Adam and God in Book 8 concerning equal companionship with the hierarchical emphasis at other moments in *Paradise Lost*? Milton's immense poem, we have begun to see, is rich enough to explore more than one model of sexual relations. The fact that its readers and critics have often argued passionately about Milton's representation of sexual relations, portraying the poet in divergent and conflicting ways – as patriarch, egalitarian, even feminist – suggests that his complex poem does not present a fully consistent ideal or stable perspective. Even Mary Wollstonecraft, in her famous *Vindication of the Rights of Woman* (1792), stressed Milton's "inconsistencies" by contrasting the patriarchal passage discussed above, in which Eve calls Adam her "Author and Disposer," with those remarkable lines in Book 8 (381–92) where Adam speaks to his maker about his need for an equal – a passage in which "Milton seems to coincide with me," Wollstonecraft noted (ch. 2). To avoid reductionism on the issue of sexual relations and politics in *Paradise Lost*, we too need to be particularly alert to its subtleties, as well as to its tensions and ambiguities.

What then happens to human sexuality and relations after the Fall itself? For one thing, as we shall see further in section 18, the marriage is redefined in the fallen world so that Adam and Eve are no longer one flesh and one spirit – only one flesh, the oneness shared with animals. Until the Fall, their sexual love and spiritual companionship had been mutually enriching (see e.g. 8.596ff.). At the Fall the forbidden fruit itself, with its aphrodisiac effect on Adam and Eve, immediately incites their "carnal desire" (9.1013), even as they benightedly fancy a new sense of divinity within them. The narrator's sharp, Augustinian language of judgement points to a dramatic change in their sexual relations, whose passion and emotional fulfillment he had valorized so glowingly in Book 4:

> hee on *Eve*
> Began to cast lascivious Eyes, she him
> As wantonly repaid; in Lust they burn.   (9.1013–15)

After wishing that there were in fact ten forbidden trees and observing the terrific effect of this drug, which inflames his sexual desire as never before, Adam seizes Eve's hand, though without his former gentleness (see 4.488–9): in the fallen world, the pleasures of "sweet reluctant amorous delay" are significantly absent from their sexual relations. Milton's gustatory metaphor for Adam and Eve's postlapsarian physical sex equates their lust with an intemperate meal:

> There they thir fill of Love and Love's disport
> Took largely, of thir mutual guilt the Seal,
> The solace of thir sin . . .   (9.1042–4)

Their fallen sexual activity serves, in effect, as a kind of "Seal" for their new marriage, a relationship constituted now on the very basis of the crime and guilt which they share. In this way, fallen sexuality, which takes on an almost libertine and pornographic quality, parodies the richness, ardor, and intense mutuality of prelapsarian sexuality and passion. Adam and Eve not only fall into burning lust, but, as we shall see later (section 18), into the destructive emotions which characterize their tormented postlapsarian relationship and which the poem's closing books will attempt to heal.

15 The material cosmos of *Paradise Lost*

In *Paradise Lost*, the unorthodox Protestant poet boldly imagines a heterodox and tangible universe. His poem presents a complex vision of his heretical monism: as we began to see in section 5, Milton believes in creation *ex materia* rather than creation *ex nihilo*. While original matter may indeed have been "a confused and disordered state at first . . . afterwards God made it ordered and beautiful" (YP 6:308). In *Paradise Lost*, Uriel, one of the angels present at the Creation, describes how it occurred:

> I saw when at his Word the formless Mass,
> This world's material mould, came to a heap:
> Confusion heard his voice, and wild uproar
> Stood rul'd, stood vast infinitude confin'd;
> Till at his second bidding darkness fled,
> Light shown, and order from disorder sprung.   (3.708–13)

Creation, then, is not from a void but from primal matter which God infuses with his vitality. The account of the Creation in Book 7 confirms Uriel's story: "Thus God the Heav'n created, thus the Earth, / Matter unform'd and void" as the Spirit infused "vital virtue" and "vital warmth / Throughout the fluid Mass" (232–7). Milton's materialism is essential to the imaginative world of *Paradise Lost*, where orthodox dualisms are continually challenged and where Milton instead envisions a tangible universe interconnected by "various degrees / Of substance" (5.473–4). Lucretius' ancient poem *De Rerum Natura* ("On the Nature of Things" [*c.* 55 BC]) was likewise concerned with a materialistic philosophy and with the material nature of the universe and all being. Milton's vital materialism, however, highlights his poem's heterodoxy in relation to traditional Christianity. Indeed, *Paradise Lost* everywhere breaks down the orthodox Christian division between matter and spirit; instead, the poem imaginatively explores their interconnection and suggests Milton's this-worldly perspective.

Paradise Lost illustrates the nature of Milton's material cosmos with great inventiveness, especially in the philosophical and scientific discourse that occurs between the sociable angel Raphael and Adam in the garden in Book 5. This discourse underscores the dynamism of Milton's Paradise by exploring the relation of spirit to matter, earth to heaven, and the phenomenal world to the world of ideas. Raphael has been sent down to earth to educate Adam and Eve in the meaning of their unfallen freedom and their happy existence in Paradise. This first education, which takes place from noon until sunset, begins with a delicious natural meal artfully prepared by Eve (5.326ff.) which the angel himself clearly enjoys, as he eats "with keen dispatch / Of real hunger" (436–7). Indeed, in Milton's organic Heaven, we later learn, the material angels enjoy great feasts, which include the delicious fruits that grow there (see 5.632ff.). Milton realizes perfectly well that this representation of corporeal angelic behavior diverges from Christian orthodoxy: the appearance and keen appetite of the angel will not conform to "the common gloss / Of Theologians" (435–6) nor to conventional angelology in his age. Milton goes out of his way here to emphasize the materiality of his angels. Man and angel share substance between them, and, as Raphael explains, angels also digest as they "Tasting concoct . . . assimilate, / And corporeal to incorporeal turn" (412–13) and even excrete what they cannot use: "what redounds, transpires / Through Spirits with ease" (438–9)! Since "Knowledge is as food" (7.126ff.) in this poem, temperate eating and the process of digestion – human, angelic, as well as cosmic (see 5.415ff. and 7.359–62) – become resonant metaphors in *Paradise Lost* for understanding one's ontology and place in a dynamic universe where matter and spirit are interconnected.

"One first matter all" proceeding from God (5.469ff.), then, is the essential lesson regarding vital materialism in this heterodox universe. The angel explains how the cosmos is a system of interdependent degrees enabling the body to work its way up to spirit, itself a state of rarified matter. To convey this dynamic material process to Adam, Raphael uses the highly apt metaphor, especially given their garden setting, of a growing plant (as did Lucretius himself in *De Rerum Natura* 1.351–7):

> So from the root
> Springs lighter the green stalk, from thence the leaves
> More aery, last the bright consummate flow'r
> Spirits odorous breathes.   (5.479–82)

Then drawing on the language of alchemy, the angel explains how "flow's and thir fruit / Man's nourishment, by gradual scale *sublim'd* / To vital spirits aspire, to animal, / To intellectual" (482–5; emphasis added), so that on this materialist ladder the highest of spirits is the intellectual (the materialist embodiment of reason). Indeed, the difference between humans and angels in terms of both substance and mode of reasoning is really only a matter of "degree, of kind the same," since, in terms of intellect, humans are more "Discursive" and angels more "Intuitive" (487–90). And so Raphael teaches Adam about the materiality of the spirit world.

The natural fact or lesson of Raphael's philosophical discourse on substance and diet – and the angel tells Adam to "Wonder not" – is that humans may in time become more and more like angels:

> And from these corporal nutriments perhaps
> Your bodies may at last turn all to spirit,
> Improv'd by tract of time, and wing'd ascend
> Ethereal, as wee.   (496–9)

This will happen, of course, only "If" the patient Adam and Eve "be found obedient" (501) – the angel's use of the conditional is crucial here. What is clear from Raphael's discourse, however, is that the importance of remaining obedient (this applies to angels as well: see 5.535–7) does not mean that one's place in the natural scale or hierarchical order is fixed or immutable. To the contrary, the universe, like Milton's Paradise itself, remains dynamic and subject to change. And in a universe where earth genuinely shares some of the delights of Heaven, and where matter is finally indistinct from spirit, it is possible for the unfallen Adam to imagine gradually and naturally acquiring an angel's spiritual body.

Clearly the blind poet of *Paradise Lost* wants the reader to admire the angel's body, which is less frail and "more refin'd" (5.475) than its human counterpart. Thus when Satan is wounded by Michael during the heavenly war, Raphael tells Adam and Eve that

> Spirits that live throughout
> Vital in every part, not as frail man
> In Entrails, Heart or Head, Liver or Reins,
> Cannot but by annihilating die;
> . . .
> All Heart they live, all Head, all Eye, All Ear,
> All Intellect, all Sense, and as they please,
> They Limb themselves.   (6.344–52)

One advantage of the angel body, which we have seen is indeed made of matter, is that it has unusual flexibility: "so soft / And uncompounded is thir Essence pure / Not ti'd or manacl'd with joint or limb" (1.424ff.) that Milton's angels can easily change shape and size, as well as sex, and do not have to worry about "the brittle strength of bones." The poet's fascination with angelic physiology and ontology accords then with his vital monism: in his tangible cosmos where one's place is earned "by degrees of merit" (7.157) and where spirit and matter are interconnected, unfallen mankind might have eventually enjoyed the benefits of angelic existence, including the advantages of an angel's body – a body turned "all to spirit." The corporeal angels in this unorthodox Protestant poem, after all, enjoy a more refined, complete form of sexual union since they experience no physical "obstacle" when they make love and can mix thoroughly, as Raphael admits as he blushes in an unfallen manner at the end of Book 8 (618ff.).

For all their apparent differences – "yet what compare?" Adam wonders (5.467) – earth may resemble the materialist Heaven even more than Adam and Eve realize. "O Earth, how like to Heav'n . . .!" (9.99) Satan himself will exclaim when he lands in Paradise in Book 9. This likeness between the terrestrial and celestial worlds is one of the last points Raphael touches on before he begins his narrative of the rebellion and war in Heaven:

> yet for thy good
> This is dispens't, and what surmounts the reach
> Of human sense, I shall delineate so,
> By lik'ning spiritual to corporal forms,
> As may express them best, though what if Earth
> Be but the shadow of Heav'n, and things therein
> Each to other like more than on Earth is thought?   (5.570–6)

The angel's language here is essentially Neoplatonic: since the phenomenal world is a "shadow" or simulacrum of Heaven, that supermundane reality, language and metaphor (like that of the angel's growing plant) become the means of accommodation between these two realms, of expressing that likeness between the corporeal and the spiritual. And so by likening "spiritual to corporal forms," Milton's own inspired poetry in *Paradise Lost* has created an astonishingly original and heterodox universe, one that breaks down traditional Christian dualisms and enables the reader to envision the similarities between Heaven and earth, spirit and matter, body and soul, angel and man – "Differing but in degree, of kind the same."

16 War in Heaven

The angel Raphael addresses Adam's desire for further knowledge by also narrating the wondrous history of Satan's great rebellion and the war in Heaven in Books 5 and 6. This epic story of celestial conflict is intended to educate Adam and Eve about the power and seductive nature of evil, the tragic consequences of not standing firm, and the meaning of obedience and godly service in a universe where all God's creatures are free to fall: "let it profit thee to have heard / By terrible Example the reward / Of disobedience" (6.909–11). The rebellion and celestial war thus refocus our attention on those central themes announced at the very opening of the poem – disobedience and loss. The first section of Raphael's narrative also enables Milton to introduce Abdiel, "Servant of God" (the meaning of his name in Hebrew): the zealous Protestant angel's vehement responses to Satan powerfully dramatize the meaning of voluntary obedience, as he dares to resist Satan's rhetoric, artifice, and conspiracy, despite the fact that he receives only hostile scorn for his bold dissent. The confrontation between Satan and Abdiel at the end of Book 5 is a particularly charged moment in *Paradise Lost*. Not only does it redefine the nature of heroic behavior in a poem that otherwise seems subversive of classical heroic ideology, but it also dramatizes political issues and rhetoric Milton confronted in his own tumultuous age.

The Son's exaltation on account of his "Merit" rather than his birthright (as God makes clear at 3.308–14) provokes the prideful and politically ambitious Satan's envy, disdain, and malice (see 5.661ff.). Milton thus gives Satan a plausible motive and cause for his resentment and revolt; with his formidable gifts as a rhetorician and cunning politician, he then uses secrecy, "Ambiguous words" (5.703), lies, and "calumnious Art" (770) to win over a third of the angels to his side. And this occurs even though Milton's Satan, before his fall, already holds a notably high position in Heaven – "great in Power, / In favor and preeminence" (5.660–1). But then as the conspiracy in Heaven shows, Satan manifests what the outstanding political philosopher of Milton's age, Thomas Hobbes, described in his *Leviathan* (1651) as "a perpetuall and restlesse desire of Power after power" (ch. 11).

Satan's political arguments and language prove contradictory, however: in one sense he speaks like a righteous revolutionary, despising the thought of submitting to "prostration vile" and bending the "supple knee" in homage to the Son's "image," while urging his compatriots "to cast off this Yoke" (5.780ff.). Yet for all his hatred of authority and idolatrous adoration, Satan also appeals to "these magnific Titles" which bestow power on the angels – "those Imperial Titles which assert / Our being ordain'd to govern, not to serve" (5.801–2). Satan's claim that title itself insures the right to power and authority is hardly the argument that a genuine revolutionary would have made in Milton's age; to the contrary, it is, as he sits exalted on his "Royal seat" (5.756), the sort of political claim we might associate with a royalist apologist. For all his posturing and presentation of himself as a heroic "Patron of liberty," we know from the angel Gabriel that in Heaven Satan behaved like the most obsequious and unctuous of flatterers: "who more than thou / Once fawn'd, and cring'd, and servilely ador'd / Heav'n's awful Monarch" (4.958–60). A consummate actor and rhetorician, the protean Satan simulates contradictory kinds of political rhetoric in his attempt to usurp power.

In Heaven only the angel Abdiel is singular and courageous in his immediate defiance of Satan's rebellious rhetoric, actions, guile, and subtlety: though he dares to call Satan's argument "blasphemous, false and proud," he finds himself alone in his resistance and zeal, as though such a response were "out of season judg'd" (5.850). In his solitary heroism, fearlessness, and trial, Abdiel resembles the daring poet himself, for he speaks boldly, "though alone / Encompass'd round with foes" (5.875–6), much like Milton who movingly describes how he sings "unchang'd" while he is "fall'n on evil days, / . . . and with dangers compast round" (7.24–8). Abdiel is likewise an archetype of the godly or just men who will emerge in Michael's panorama of human history; such biblical figures as Enoch, Noah, Abraham, Moses, Joshua, and a few others will stand out as the "righteous in a World perverse" (11.701), which Adam learns about in the poem's final books. "Unmov'd / Unshak'n, unseduc'd, unterrifi'd" (5.898–9), Abdiel displays the negative heroism of Sonnet 19 – "They also serve who only stand and wait" – as well as the solitary heroism of Milton's Jesus in *Paradise Regained*, who likewise chooses to remain unmoved despite Satan's skillful rhetoric, his numerous verbal assaults and temptations. Abdiel embodies the singleness of truth confronting the multiplicity of falsehood. His trial is clearly an example to Adam and Eve (one that has important implications for the events of Book 9) of what it means for the godly individual to stand firm in the midst of temptation. Indeed, although Satan is engaged in promoting rebellion against God's authority, it is the steadfast Abdiel who, in Satan's view, behaves like the "seditious Angel" (6.152): this is the only instance where a character uses the inflammatory epithet "seditious." Here Satan manipulates the language of political rebellion for his own ends – to slander his fearless challenger. Milton is aware of the often equivocal nature of such highly charged political language – of the ways it can be exploited by usurpers themselves.

Milton's God, we have seen, puts all his servants to the test and his loyal angels are no exception. In the martial epic of Book 6, their faith is tried by a war which they by themselves do not win, even with the help of the prophetic Michael; unlike the heroes of a classical epic, they win no martial honor or renown, though they do stand firm in their loyalty and manifest "Heroic Ardor" (6.66). Milton's war in Heaven is nothing less than a civil war where the loyal angels fearlessly fight a "righteous Cause" (6.804) as "armed Saints" (6.47; cf. 767) – that is, as Puritan-style saints fighting a holy war of truth against Satan's forces who have chosen of their own free will to revolt. Indeed, such loyal and zealous warring saints in Heaven prefigure those faithful Protestant saints who will fight the godly wars of truth on earth.

The battle in Heaven is based on Revelation 12:7–9, where Michael and his angels war against the dragon or Satan and his apostate angels and cast them out of Heaven. Milton, however, has once again greatly elaborated his Biblical source. He presents the battle with Satan as a disturbing, cataclysmic confrontation that is both cosmic and epic in its scope and character: "all Heav'n / Resounded, and had Earth been then, all Earth / Had to her Centre shook" (6.217–19). It is a fierce war which lasts three days and in which the landscape of Heaven itself is torn up and ravaged. At the end of the second day of battle there is still no resolution to the "horrid confusion" (6.668) and Milton suggests the futility of continual warfare:

> Whence in perpetual fight they needs must last
> Endless, and no solution will be found:
> War wearied hath perform'd what War can do.   (6.693–5)

It is at this point, on the third day, that the Son himself (rather than the archangel Michael), expressing the vehemence and wrath of the Father, defeats the rebel angels who are hurled down to "the bottomless pit," highlighting the apocalyptic dimensions of the heavenly conflict and recalling the punishment of Satan in Revelation 20:3.

In this great war, Michael's mighty sword of prophecy and judgement (like the prophetic sword in Rev. 19:15) may remind us of the famous "two-handed engine" in *Lycidas*, and its association with terrifying apocalyptic judgement, as the angel battles Satan's forces "with huge two-handed sway" (6.251). Satan's forces, who "by [physical] strength / ... measure all" (6.820–1), as the Son observes, fight an epic-style war in Heaven. Although they do not face the risk of human mortality, as ancient Greek fighters do, their martial values and heroic ideology are nevertheless largely Homeric: this epic military struggle they "style / The strife of Glory" (6.289–90), as they attack the forces of "The Thunderer" (an epithet recalling the power of the Olympian Zeus) and pursue "Honor, Dominion, Glory, and renown" (6.491, 422). And when Satan and Michael confront each other during the first day of battle, they seem like Homeric gods or warriors "in stature, motion, arms / Fit to decide the Empire of great Heav'n" (6.302–3). Even when Satan is wounded, he feels a sense of "shame" (6.340), exactly what the intensely competitive epic hero, who lives in a "shame culture" valorizing warlike heroism, wants to avoid at all costs. As the Lycian warrior Glaucus relates in Book 6 of the *Iliad*, when he was sent to Troy, he was commanded "to act always with valor, / always to be most noble, never to shame / the line of [his] progenitors" (trans. Robert Fitzgerald). Indeed, Milton associates Satan and his host with such epic militancy only to suggest that its heroic values are outmoded. The duel with Michael, which momentarily humbles Satan's pride when he is wounded, remains inconclusive and Satan wins no personal glory from it. Warfare, in its brutality, glory, and competitiveness, is of course one of the great subjects of epic (the *Iliad* is especially dominated by it), and so Milton places the battle for the territory of God at the center of his own epic poem; such Renaissance poets as Tasso, Vida, and Phineas Fletcher had also made celestial warfare central to their works. But Milton does so in order to explode the martial values of epic poetry and to reveal the limitations of its outmoded heroic ideology and code, as he himself raises the name of epic to something higher and more visionary.

The competitive and scheming Satan does not only fight a heroic war based on prowess, however; he also fights, on the second day, a modern-style war with gunpowder and cannons, whose power and fury both test and humiliate God's faithful angels. Satan is a technocrat who uses the techniques of mining to get at the "materials dark and crude" in Heaven's "Entrails" (reminding the poem's readers again of Heaven's likeness to earth), so as to invent the hellish weapons of Renaissance and modern warfare – another product of his perverse creativity. This military creativity reverses the movement from matter to spirit so elaborately detailed in Raphael's discourse in Book 5, for Satan transforms purity into filth, and his firing cannons are described in vivid scatological language:

> Immediate in a flame,
> But soon obscur'd with smoke, all Heav'n appear'd,
> From those deep-throated Engines belcht, whose roar
> Embowell'd with outrageous noise the Air,
> And all her entrails tore, disgorging foul
> Thir devilish glut.   (6.584–9)

In the Sin and Death passage of Book 2, we recall, Milton had rendered in grotesque imagery the equally grotesque violence and hatred towards one's provider and creator by describing the monstrous dogs gnawing at Sin's bowels. Here, the description characterizes the belching cannons in terms of the violent rejection of food, as Satan likewise furiously turns against his creator. Satan is the anal devil – dark, filthy, noisy. (One might think of the scatological depictions of war machinery in the nightmarish paintings of Hieronymus Bosch.) Indeed, Milton's portrayal of his weapons in these terms reverses the angel's earlier lesson of good eating and nourishment. Satan's belching cannons, whose great roar reduces words to "barbarous dissonance" (7.32), express his crude sensibility and destructive imagination.

The great performance and final heroic act in this apocalyptic drama of heavenly conflict, however, is reserved not for the loyal warring angels (who suffer a number of setbacks and do not win a decisive victory), nor for the warring archangel Michael (as was often the case in other Renaissance poems about angelic warfare), but for the Son of God himself who receives the transfusion of God's potent light (6.719–22). The Son's power and energy on the third day of the war again exemplify that major Miltonic theme of strength made perfect in the weakness of humility. Above the archangels but subordinate to God, the Son, unlike Satan, willingly *chooses* to serve, delighting in his act of obedience, as he manifests in *Paradise Lost* the Father's creative potency, wrath, and mildness. The last day of the war in Heaven is completely given over to his apocalyptic triumph as he assumes not the armor of a classical warrior, but the radiant and righteous armor of God (see 2 Cor. 6:7 and Eph. 6:13). His victory itself, including his ascendancy over Satan, is eschatological in force, anticipating the day of the Lord's coming and the Last Judgement (see 6.742ff.). The conquering Son ascends at the center of the poem ("Ascended" [6.762] is the central word in the 1667 edition) in a visionary triumphal chariot based on Ezekiel 1:4–6 and recalling the imagery of the Apocalypse (e.g. Rev. 4:8). With its whirlwind, flames, and smoke, it is both sublime and terrifying, symbolic of the warring Son's glory and power:

> forth rush'd with whirl-wind sound
> The Chariot of Paternal Deity,
> Flashing thick flames, Wheel within Wheel, undrawn,
> Itself instinct with Spirit, but convoy'd
> By four Cherubic shapes, four Faces each
> Had wondrous, as with Stars thir bodies all
> And Wings were set with Eyes, with Eyes the Wheels
> Of Beryl, and careering Fires between.   (6.749–56)

This sublime and self-propelled chariot, which thoroughly transcends its traditional epic counterpart, conveys immense energy and inexorable force; and it does so in a way that is poetically vivid. In Milton's tract, *An Apology for Smectymnuus*, vehemence itself is associated with the figure of the militant and apocalyptic "Zeale" who "ascends his fiery Chariot drawn with two blazing Meteors figur'd like beasts . . . resembling two of those four which *Ezechiel* and *S. John* saw, the one visag'd like a Lion to expresse power, high autority and indignation, the other of count'nance like a man to cast derision and scorne upon perverse and fraudulent seducers" (YP 1:900). So, too, in Book 6 of *Paradise Lost*, sacred vehemence and indignation assume visionary form in the apocalyptic Chariot of Paternal Deity in which, Raphael tells us, "every eye / Glar'd lightning, and shot forth pernicious fire / Among th' accurst" (6.848–50). Overcome by the mighty power and wrath of God (different, as we have seen, from pagan wrath), Satan and the rebel angels are given no heroic exit from Heaven as they are driven out "as a Herd / Of Goats or timorous flock" (856–7); thus they fall flaming for nine days through Chaos until they reach Hell, the infernal place where Milton began, *in medias res*, his great epic story. And so the first half of *Paradise Lost* ends with the expulsion of Satan from Heaven, just as the second half of the poem will end with the expulsion of man from Eden.

17 Creation

With the conclusion of the war in Heaven, Milton signals in his invocation to Book 7 that he has finished the first half of his ambitious poem, thereby calling attention to his work's elegant symmetry – "Half yet remains unsung" (7.21). The second half of *Paradise Lost* (from Books 7 to 12) begins with the Creation and ends with the Apocalypse, exactly like the Bible itself. Moreover, the central books of the poem – Books 6 and 7 – elaborate the poem's opening themes of disobedience and loss followed, after that pivotal word "till" (1.4) in the first invocation, by the theme of restoration ("till one greater Man / Restore us"). Thus having narrated the destruction and fall dramatized in the war in Heaven, Raphael's historiographical discourse turns to the primal subject of the Creation itself – to God's making of the new world and man. And so following the martial epic of Book 6, which we have seen Milton reform to suit his visionary poem, the poet gives us in Book 7 a brief Creation or hexaemeral epic (a genre popularized by the sixteenth-century French poet Du Bartas), a narrative which imaginatively displays God's creative energy and vital power, as it highlights the poem's themes of renewal and vitality.

Indeed, in Raphael's hexaemeral epic the Son himself appears in a different role: we no longer see him as the militant figure who expresses the avenging wrath of God or the *odium Dei*, but rather as God's powerful Word or Logos, the agency of creation instead of destruction. This book, then, manifests another dimension of God's power as he expands "his Empire" (7.555) by creation – a contrast, clearly, to Satan's imperial ambitions. The Son himself, moreover, is even greater in his acts of creation than he is in his glorious conquest of the ungodly angels, since "to create / Is greater than created to destroy" (7.606–7). (Significantly, Satan is absent from this book, as well as the next one.) The creative work of God, while it may require Raphael "to descend" (7.84) from the martial exploits of celestial warfare, is in fact a more wondrous, exalted subject for this visionary epic, one that tests the angel's narrative powers:

"to recount Almighty works / What words or tongue of Seraph can suffice, / Or heart of man suffice to comprehend?" (7.112–14). Milton's emphasis in this Biblical-style book based on Genesis is on the wonder, potency, and diversity of God's dynamic creation. The poetic language and rhetorical descriptions attempt to convey precisely these qualities and in a way that is accommodated to human understanding – "so told," in the angel's narrative, "as earthly notion can receive" (7.179).

We have already seen that Milton wholly rejects the notion of creation *ex nihilo*, emphasizing instead the Spirit of God's active infusion of vital virtue and life into fluid matter as he purges downward (we may think of Satan here) "The black tartareous cold Infernal dregs / Adverse to life" (7.238–9). Milton's diction as he describes the dynamic forces of creation is essentially Biblical; his vivid poetic language captures the abundance, motion, and energy of creation as he describes how on the newly-formed and fruitful earth

> Forth flourish'd thick the clustr'ing Vine, forth crept
> The smelling Gourd, up stood the corny Reed
> Embattl'd in her field: and th' humble Shrub,
> And Bush with frizzl'd hair implicit: last
> Rose as in Dance the stately Trees, and spread
> Thir branches hung with copious Fruit: or gemm'd
> Thir Blossoms.   (7.320–6)

Milton's graphic details and dynamic verbs convey the vigor and sensuous particularity of the process of divine creation; if the "stately trees" seem to dance, so do the stars (7.373ff.), likewise expressing the vibrant energy of God's creation. Even light in its "quintessence pure / *Sprung* from the Deep" (7.244–45), while the huge mountains "thir broad bare backs *upheave* / Into the Clouds" (286–7; emphasis added): Milton's active verbs convey vitality, as well as divine potency. On the sixth day of God's creative work, the animals, themselves bursting with life, express a sense of primal energy and newly-found freedom – "The Tawny Lion, pawing to get free / His hinder parts, then springs as broke from Bonds" (7.464–5).

Moreover, the fecundity and energy associated with divine creation and sexual generation is everywhere present in this book (thus making Raphael's creation story particularly accessible to the experience of Adam and Eve), as well as in other passages of *Paradise Lost*. Milton vividly describes how the earth "Op'ning her fertile Womb teem'd at a birth/ Innumerous living Creatures . . ." (7.453ff.; cf. 276ff.), thus generating the animals. This emphasis on the fertility of creation is of course already there from the very beginning of the poem, where Milton describes how the Holy Spirit present at the genesis "Dove-like satst brooding on the vast Abyss / and mad'st it pregnant" (1.21–2). And indeed Milton's universe is itself animated by sexual energy: at the time of Raphael's entrance in Book 5, "the mounted Sun / Shot down direct his fervid Rays, to warm / Earth's inmost womb," while "Nature here / Wanton'd as in her prime" (300–2, 294–5). Elsewhere Raphael will explain to Adam, again describing a sexually animated universe, that the sun and the moon communicate "Male and Female Light, / Which two great Sexes animate the World" (8.150–1).

Once Adam's "thirst" (8.8) for knowledge of the Creation and its wonders has been satisfied (in this poem man, unlike the devils, is not tantalized), there is still the further question of the design of the universe and its celestial motions – one of the subjects of the discourse between man and angel in Book 8. But one of Raphael's concerns in Book 7's creation account has been to satisfy fully the "desire / Of knowledge *within bounds*" (7.119–20; emphasis added). This is a poem that, despite its ambitious theme of pursuing things unattempted and soaring with no middle flight, emphasizes the value of being "lowly wise" (8.173) and of not speculating too high. As Raphael tells Adam, "Heav'n is for thee too high / To know what passes there" (8.172–3): knowing about the Creation is one thing, but speculating randomly about matters regarding "highest Heav'n" (8.178) is quite another. *Paradise Lost* remains a this-worldly poem, ambiguous about dreaming of "matters hid" (8.167) and, consequently, when it comes to the astronomical constitution of the "Fabric of the Heav'ns" (8.76), it never settles firmly on one model – Ptolemaic or Copernican. It certainly raises the possibility of a Copernican or heliocentric conception of the heavens ("What if the Sun / Be Centre to the World . . ." [8.122ff.]), though Milton skillfully avoids committing himself on this issue. Adam, then, finds himself thoroughly educated in the dynamic history of the Creation, but he is also warned that it is indeed dangerous to "err in things too high" (8.121). And so it is the prime wisdom that "lies in daily life" (8.193) that this poem ultimately valorizes, despite its creator's bold desire to "see and tell / Of things invisible to mortal sight" (3.54–5).

18 The tragedy of the Fall

Unlike other epic poets, Milton makes central to his great mythic narrative a domestic tragedy, as he attempts to retell freshly the original story of the Fall. From the terse, elliptical hints of Genesis, Milton brilliantly elaborates a tragic drama of separation, temptation, and falling, followed by man's terrible psychological and emotional torment. This modulation to tragedy in *Paradise Lost* constitutes a firm break in its design, as the poet makes clear in his proem to Book 9: he "must change / Those Notes to Tragic" (5–6), now that the poetic hexaemeron of Book 7, as well as the philosophical, intellectual, and social discourse between man and angel are finished. Milton's generic shift here – as he emphasizes his "Sad task" (9.13) – reminds us that the work was itself originally conceived as tragic drama (see section 1). With Book 9, moreover, Milton picks up the narrative thread which he left off at Book 4 in order to insert Raphael's divine historiography and account of cosmic creation (Books 5–8). From Book 9 on, *Paradise Lost* will develop the tragic story, as well as the immediate and larger historical consequences of Satan's mission of destructive revenge.

Yet while this Christian tragedy will involve sharp judgement – "distaste, / Anger and just rebuke" (9.9–10) on Heaven's part – it also engages the emotional sympathy of the poet who injects his own personal responses into the tragic narrative of temptation and loss: "O much deceiv'd, much failing, hapless *Eve* . . ." Milton treats the Fall with great pathos and feeling, though his poem repeatedly reminds us that there is no doubt that Adam and Eve were wrong – the sole and simple prohibition was "easy" as Adam himself tells Eve (4.433) and as the narrator himself suggests in Book 7 ("that sole command, / So easily obey'd," 47–8). The fruit itself – a thing neither good nor evil – was symbolic of their obedience freely observed: "It was necessary" Milton writes in his *Christian Doctrine*, "that one thing at least should be either forbidden or commanded, and above all something which was in itself neither good nor evil, so that man's obedience might in this way be made evident" (YP 6:351–2). In the process of the temptation, however, Eve is deceived (though she already knows about the danger and prohibition: see 9.274ff., 651ff.), while Adam, Milton makes clear, following scriptural authority (1 Tim. 2:14), is not (9.998): Adam in this sense is the more culpable partner. Yet the tragic fall of our primal mother and father does differ in important ways from the terrible and Titanic fall of Satan: their disobedience or rebellion is not, after all, prompted by meditated revenge, willful maliciousness or hatred; and unlike the rebel angels, their fall is not brought on "by thir own suggestion" as if they were "Self-tempted, self-deprav'd" (3.129–30).

It is important to notice, furthermore, that Adam and Eve remain unfallen until the Fall itself. Eve is "yet sinless" (9.659) the poet observes as the serpent's skillful arguments are beginning to win their way into her imagination. Earlier critical moments in the poem – Eve's potential narcissism at the pool, which she relates in her autobiography (4.440ff.), and her troubling Satanic dream, which she describes to Adam at the beginning of Book 5 – do not themselves indicate her fallenness and guilt (as commentators sometimes suggest). They do reveal, however, that Eve is fallible and capable of sinning.

In making the domestic drama between Adam and Eve central, Milton's poem delicately registers emotional tensions which exist even in the unfallen state. Their marital debate (a scene Milton has invented) revolves at first around economic efficiency: Eve believes that the best way to contain the "wanton growth" of the garden is to divide their labors and to separate work from pleasure since less gets done with amorous distractions; Adam, however, disagrees, arguing that such "sweet intercourse" (like the sensuous pleasure of "sweet reluctant amorous delay") is a higher form of food and that their labor is not to be measured quantitatively. Adam may have a good point, but his subsequent supercilious and uxorious platitude hardly endears him to our original mother nor to many of the poem's readers: "The Wife, where danger or dishonor lurks, / Safest and seemliest by her Husband stays" (9.267–8), he pompously states, hurting Eve's feelings and prompting her to stand on her own dignity and assert her sense of independence – her ability to remain firm on her own in the face of temptation from their adversary. Milton's domestic drama thus enables the poet to explain why Eve was alone when the serpent tempted her (Genesis is ambiguous on this point, as we have noted).

In a sense Eve has the better argument in the crucial pre-temptation dispute. It seems as if she has read Milton's own *Areopagitica*, or at least already understands one of its essential themes, and knows that "Virtue unassay'd" (9.335) is meaningless, while Adam, trying to soothe Eve with "healing words" (290), goes on to make a weak argument about temptation:

> For hee who tempts, though in vain, at least asperses
> The tempted with dishonor foul, suppos'd
> Not incorruptible of Faith, not proof
> Against temptation.   (296–9)

But Milton, whose *Areopagitica* rejected a "cloistered vertue . . . that never sallies out and sees her adversary" (as we saw in section 3), would hardly agree with Adam's point that temptation, even when it fails, brings dishonor to the individual tempted; indeed, Milton passionately defended temptation by trial since what "purifies us is triall." In both his prose and verse, Milton valorizes confrontation and conflict, and *Paradise Lost*, which defines virtue in the context of evil, shows the need for truth and falsehood to grapple. To be sure, Adam is right to stress that the cunning, verbally skillful enemy who could seduce angels could very well seduce Eve and deceive "Reason"; but Adam's argument that he must see her in order to know that she is in fact tempted – "th' other who can know, / Not seeing thee attempted, who attest?" (368–9) – is itself unpersuasive.

Yet fearing Eve's displeasure, he abandons his authority at this point – he, after all, does not wish to compromise her free choice – as he reluctantly lets her go, while hoping that she will stay: "Go; for thy stay, not free, absents thee more" (9.372). The superb intervention of the narrator, with its carefully positioned words, underscores the psychological and emotional tension of the moment, suggesting Eve's own contradictory impulses: "So spake the Patriarch of Mankind, but *Eve* / Persisted, yet submiss, though last, repli'd" (9.376–7). When the narrator intervenes again, a few lines later, his anguished lament will underscore the tragedy of the "event perverse" (404ff.), as well as his deep sympathy and personal feeling as he narrates his epic story of the Fall.

As Milton carefully prepares us for the temptation scene itself, he includes telling details which portray Eve as both attractive and vulnerable. He calls attention significantly to her hand which "Soft she withdrew" (9.386) from Adam's: this, then, is the last time Adam and Eve hold hands (symbolic of marriage and concord) as an unfallen couple; indeed, it is Satan who will next see her hand (9.438). Moreover, the mythic comparisons Milton introduces, as unfallen Eve departs with her gardening tools, are telling (see 9.386ff.): her beauty outdoes even that of Diana, the goddess of woodland and wild nature. But Milton also conveys a more ominous sense of feminine beauty menaced when he alludes, for instance, to the seduction of Pomona (the Roman goddess of fruit) by the god Vertumnus, who assumed various shapes (as in Ovid's *Metamorphoses*, Book 14), and to the incestuous seduction of the beautiful Proserpina (daughter of Ceres) by Jove in the shape of a serpent. The poet likewise suggests Eve's attractiveness and vulnerability when he describes her in pastoral and elegiac terms at the moment Satan discovers her alone (see 9.423–33). A complex simile comparing Satan to a pent-up city dweller going out into the pleasant countryside (445ff.) reinforces further the contrast between Eve's pastoral innocence and his active malice, manifested as well in his misogynist and (last) dramatic soliloquy preceding his temptation in the "pleasing" and ambiguous "shape" (9.503) of the serpent.

The tempter's slick appeal, however, is not only visual, as he attempts "To lure her Eye" (9.518); it is also rhetorical: "list'n not to his Temptations" (6.908), Raphael had warned. But here the rhetoric differs considerably from the martial oratory which characterizes Satan's impressive speeches in the poem's early books. In his role as tempter, Satan begins by wooing Eve with the language of Renaissance love poetry (9.532–48), referring to her "disdain," "awful brow" and "Celestial Beauty," as though she were the beautiful but scornful lady of the Petrarchan sonnet tradition (he had used similar seductive language in her dream: 5.43ff.). And he addresses her as a "Goddess" and "Empress" – and later even by the daring oxymoron "Goddess humane" (9.732) – extravagant titles meant to provoke the vulnerable Eve (who tends towards vanity, while Adam tends towards uxoriousness) to aspire beyond her human condition to female sovereignty and godhead.

The most brilliant feature of Satan's temptation, however, is his autobiographical narrative (9.571ff.), the last autobiography in the poem (Eve has hers in Book 4 and Adam his in Book 8) and a passage that is one of Milton's most imaginative additions to the Biblical story. For here Satan essentially tells a fictional story of self-creation – how he rose a notch in the chain of being by eating the alluring fruit. Just as the goodly tree nourished him – satisfying his keen appetite while all other "envying" creatures were tantalized – so it can nourish Eve. Indeed, his desire satisfied, Satan perceived a "Strange alteration," gained human speech, and began to engage in "Speculations high or deep" – the very kind that Raphael dismissed as unfruitful in Book 8. Satan's account of his transformation, moreover, parodies (as does 9.713ff.) Raphael's monistic discourse describing how humankind may become more angelic; yet Satan's clever story about the miraculous power of the fruit begins to work wonders on Eve who now becomes "more amaz'd" (9.614) and allows the serpent to replace Adam as her guide as he leads her "into fraud" and to the tree, "root of all our woe" (643–5).

Though still "sinless," Eve attempts to test the serpent's truth ("Wondrous indeed, *if* cause of such effects," 9.650; emphasis added), while Satan, the self-conscious actor, responds more boldly, his rhetorical performance resembling that of some famous ancient orator from democratic Athens or the republic of Rome (9.670–8). Having parodied Raphael's discourse, Satan's speech (679ff.) now parodies Milton's own inspired invocations and theodicy as the serpent claims "to discern / Things in thir Causes" and "to trace the ways / Of highest Agents." Trivializing death itself ("whatever thing Death be") and God's prohibition ("a petty Trespass"), the deceptive Satan is beginning to lure the increasingly vulnerable Eve into a Satanic epic in which language itself is paganized: thus her "dauntless virtue" – meaning courage here – might be praised by God, and Adam and Eve in their knowledge would themselves "be as Gods." Indeed, one consequence of the Fall is that religion itself will become paganized. Fallaciously collapsing knowledge into experience ("if what is evil / Be real, why not known, since easier shunn'd?"), Satan's discourse encourages Eve to aspire to Godhead as he suggests that God's prohibition might be due to envy, a provocative suggestion that tells us more about Satan than it does about God.

Satan's skillful words at this point win "too easy entrance" (9.734ff.) into Eve's heart, suggesting his inward invasion and violation of her emotions and thoughts, as Eve gazes on the "fair" fruit and as both appetite and desire move through the ladder of the five senses (from sight to taste). Significantly, Milton adds a dramatic touch, allowing Eve to pause "a while" and muse to herself in a soliloquy before she actually takes the fruit. Convinced that the fruit is the cure of "our want" (9.755) – suggesting both desire as well as a lack (i.e. of not being God) – her speech begins to resemble Satan's, as she reveals that she is completely won over by his guile. Then, taking only two lines to narrate the key action whose tragic consequences for humankind are so immense, Milton emphasizes the loss of the voluntary in Eve's gesture: "So saying, her rash hand in evil hour / Forth reaching to the Fruit, she pluck'd, she eat" (9.780–1). The impetuosity suggested by that "rash hand" precludes careful choice as the act itself becomes a compulsion. Indeed, mother earth immediately feels the wound, just as she will later suffer a bellyache when Adam himself eats the fruit (9.1000ff.) – again linking the Fall with internal violation. The Fall is no heroic act in *Paradise Lost* and the slick serpent no great epic figure triumphant in his moment of glory ("Back to the Thicket slunk / The guilty Serpent"). The narrator's language turns bitter and ironic as he describes Eve's compulsive eating: "Greedily she ingorg'd without restraint, / And knew not eating Death . . ." One of the terrible ironies, unrecognized by our first mother of course, is that Death itself will now eat her and her children (see e.g. 10.603ff.).

Milton invests his story of the Fall with considerable pathos as he presents Eve in her next soliloquy (often in this poem a fallen form of discourse) idolizing the fair tree and giving it her maternal care (9.795ff.). The fallen Eve now shows a new concern for role-playing ("to *Adam* in what sort / Shall I appear?"), and she reveals a new sense of female inadequacy (821–4) and a fear of displacement (827–30) that convince her to share her condition with Adam. In addition, she reveals that she has fallen into a Satanic way of thinking which prompts her to wonder "for inferior who is free?". The answer of *Paradise Lost*, of course, is that all who are inferior are free, since obedience is freedom – as Raphael's story of the faithful Abdiel had amply illustrated.

Unlike Eve, Adam is not deceived at all; yet in his fall, he reveals that he too is emotionally vulnerable. He falls quickly, quite un-like the Adam in one of Milton's analogues, Hugo Grotius' tragedy *Adamus Exul* or *The Exile of Adam* (1601). There, Adam at first wa-vers as he is torn by his conflicting loves for God and Eve. But Milton's uxorious Adam cannot imagine life without Eve (9.896ff.): his part-ner is completely irreplaceable, and with her absent, he would never stop weeping ("loss of thee / Would never from my heart"). In a way, Adam's emotional response is heroic and chivalric, an example of "exceeding Love" (9.961) that recalls the behavior of the Son – though with a crucial difference: this is sacrificial love without vol-untary obedience. Moreover, the marriage itself is being redefined here. In Book 8 it had included "one Flesh, one Heart, one Soul" (499), a revision of Genesis 2:24 that stressed the remarkable de-gree of intimacy between our first parents. But here, in Book 9, that spiritual companionship is lost – "Flesh of Flesh, / Bone of my Bone thou art" (914–15; cf. 958–9). Indeed, insofar as there is any one-ness in their fallen marriage, that now entails "one Guilt, one Crime" (971). Sharing that with Eve, Adam himself becomes evasive about God's commandment and falls into Satanic thinking (see 927ff.). The poet's contemptuous description of the uxorious Adam now "fondly overcome with Female charm" (999) recalls the "pleasing sorcery" in Hell which "could charm / Pain for a while or anguish, and excite / Fallacious hope" (2.566–8).

Indeed, the fruit in Milton's story seems intoxicating so that Adam and Eve imagine themselves rising a notch; and it functions as well as an aphrodisiac, making their passion impulsive and involuntary. We have already noted what happens to human sexuality after the Fall (in section 14); but what remains to be considered are the power-ful psychological effects of the Fall. The elated intoxication Adam and Eve feel after they eat soon wears off, however, so that when they arise after their perfunctory lovemaking, they both feel a sense of terrible shame at their intemperance. Milton emphasizes their psy-chological nakedness and unrest (9.1054ff.), and he significantly does so by focusing on their faces rather than their genitals: "in our Faces evident the signs / Of foul concupiscence," as Adam bitterly observes (9.1077–8) now that he is "estrang'd in look" (1132). Milton, moreover, presents their fallen psychological state as an inner landscape of shame and despair:

> nor only Tears
> Rain'd at thir Eyes, but high Winds worse within
> Began to rise, high Passions, Anger, Hate,
> Mistrust, Suspicion, Discord, and shook sore
> Thir inward State of Mind, calm Region once
> And full of Peace, now toss't and turbulent.   (9.1121–6)

The subsequent political metaphor of inward usurpation – as appetite usurps reason (1127ff.) – anticipates inwardly the external history of tyranny which will dominate the last two books of the poem. Book 9 concludes with great bitterness between our first parents, as they, hopelessly unable to find a way out of this terrible psychological maze, speak in "alter'd style" (1132), accusing each other in the harsh colloquial tones that Milton now associates with their fallen discourse.

That bitter domestic tragedy, moreover, continues in Book 10; and yet it is also there that our original mother and father, after much painful struggle and inward torment, make peace with each other in the fallen world. Adam at first employs evasive rhetoric (see section 9), blaming Eve rather than himself, while the shameful Eve, unlike her partner, speaks directly, using Biblical diction: "The Serpent me beguil'd and I did eat" (10.162). As the heavens and earth themselves begin to show signs of change and stormy disruption, the fallen Adam himself begins to soliloquize (10.720ff.), his Job-like lament and complaint against God expressing his torment within and leading him to despair rather than to contrition. Meditating inconclusively on death and lying outstretched on the cold ground, he recalls Satan outstretched on the burning lake (see 1.209–10). The garden has become both a labyrinth and an abyss out of which the despairing Adam finds "no way" (844).

In this terrible psychological state, Adam fiercely spurns Eve, punning bitterly upon the etymology of her name: he calls her "Serpent" (the meaning of the Hebrew *Heva*; see 10.867), whereas the true Hebraic sense, which Adam will only later recover, reveals that Eve means "life" (see 11.159–60, 168–9). Indeed, it is Eve who leads

Adam out of this dark, mazelike condition. Her redeeming softness (see 10.865) triumphs over his fierce bitterness and misogynistic accusations (misogyny, Milton shows, is thus a fallen state of mind and must be judged in *Paradise Lost* according to its dramatic context):

> Forsake me not thus, *Adam*, witness Heav'n
> What love sincere, and reverence in my heart
> I bear thee, and unweeting have offended,
> Unhappily deceiv'd; thy suppliant
> I beg, and clasp thy knees . . .   (10.914ff.)

This speech marks a crucial turning point in the poem, for without Eve's heroic intervention, which establishes a new kind of heroism in the fallen world, the mutual accusations between guilty man and woman would appear to have no end at all. It is her agency that truly initiates, after the Fall, the restoration of their marriage. Like the Son in Book 3 (or even Satan in Book 2), she is the redeemer figure, the intercessor whose language of self-sacrifice especially recalls the Son's. Eve's moving speech has an immediate effect on Adam who finds himself "disarm'd" by her words (945). As the military metaphor suggests, the fruitless battle between our mother and father has finally ended; thanks to Eve, they can gradually begin to reconstitute their marriage on fallen terms. And yet the poet's tragic notes are by no means finished, as the last and starkest books of *Paradise Lost* make clear.

19 Postlapsarian history and the inner paradise

The poem's final books, where Adam is educated in postlapsarian history (for he needs, indeed, to be re-educated after the Fall), have not always been well received by critics of *Paradise Lost*. Commentators have sometimes found them less artistic and rewarding than other parts of the epic. In the eighteenth century, Joseph Addison observed that in these books "the Author has been so attentive to his Divinity, that he has neglected his Poetry" (*The Spectator*, No. 369, 1712); and in the twentieth century C. S. Lewis, perhaps their most famous detractor, called them "inartistic" and "an untransmuted lump of futurity" (*A Preface to Paradise Lost*, p. 129). These austere books are starker than previous ones in *Paradise Lost*, both in terms of their vision and their style; but then their subject matter is often dark and troubling as the archangel Michael, a less sociable spirit than Raphael, shows Adam "supernal Grace contending / With sinfulness of Men" (11.359–60), and long periods of error and superstition in human history. There is bitterness expressed in this harrowing vision of history, which further elaborates the poem's tragic dimension begun in Book 9. With the failure of the English Revolution, Milton saw his hopes for church and national reformation dashed, and these books register the poet's sense of disappointment with historical ages – including his own – dominated by men's lust for "Secular power" (12.517). But we can also read these as courageous and moving books in which the poet, in the spirit of his political writings, is not afraid (even after the Restoration) to attack tyranny or defend the authority of "those written Records pure" (12.513). In their own unsettling way, these books fulfill the critical aim of the prophetic poet, announced in his *Reason of Church-Government* (1642), "to deplore the general relapses of Kingdoms and States from justice and Gods true worship" (YP 1:817). Moreover, through a series of challenging historical lessons, Adam learns what it means to be an exile in history and the significance of the symbolic "paradise within."

Indeed, the final books emphasize the process of inward reformation: the Son speaks of God's "implanted Grace in Man" and God's "seed / Sown with contrition in his heart" (11.23, 26–7). In this Protestant epic about the inner life, then, the garden is ultimately sown within the self. (In the competitive pagan world of Homeric epic there is, by contrast, much greater emphasis on exterior actions and achievements.) And so just before Michael begins the series of historical pageants, he purges the fallen Adam's visual nerve in order that he may see more inwardly: "So deep the power of these Ingredients pierc'd, / Ev'n to the inmost seat of mental sight" (11.417–18). All of Milton's great Protestant poems emphasize interiority or what Milton calls in his later prose "the inward man and his actions" (YP 7:255): Jesus in *Paradise Regained* speaks about God's "spirit of truth" as "an inward oracle" which dwells "in pious hearts" (1.463); and when the blind Samson destroys the Philistine temple and theater, he does it paradoxically "With inward eyes illuminated" (*Samson*, 1689). So, too, Milton at the end of *Paradise Lost* emphasizes the symbolic "paradise within" – the symbol that the homeless exile in history carries within her or himself. And since, as we have seen, Milton vehemently rejects external authorities (church or state) which might force a conscience, his poem at the end suggests that the only true church itself lies within – within just men like Enoch, Noah, Abraham, and Christ.

Adam and Eve must learn the meaning of their expulsion and especially, in the spirit of *Lycidas*, learn to "weep no more" over the loss of Paradise, as they readjust their sense of place and their relation to God; like Virgil's Aeneas, they must learn to stop mourning for the past as they prepare for a new beginning. At first, Adam and Eve are too optimistic about the process of salvation and the trials of the future, concluding that "the bitterness of death / Is past" (11.157–8). The mode of banishment at the end of the poem is nevertheless temperate: "If patiently thy bidding they obey, / Dismiss them not disconsolate," God tells Michael; the double negative registers the delicate balance of emotions which characterizes their expulsion as Adam and Eve are sent forth "sorrowing, yet in peace" (11.112–13, 117: cf. 11.361). Thus, when our "ling'ring Parents" leave Paradise at the very end, the poet tells us that "Some natural tears they dropp'd, but wip'd them soon" (12.645), again underscoring the mixed emotions of loss and consolation evoked by Michael's prophecy and the prospect of exile.

Michael's prophecy includes a series of historical scenes or pageants: indeed, in the early draft of his Biblical tragedy, "Adam unparadiz'd," Milton was clearly thinking of a tragic dramatic presentation when he referred to the angel, before banishing Adam and Eve, causing "to passe before [Adam's] eyes a mask of all the evills of this life & world" (YP 8:560). This historical drama, itself a kind of Biblical epic, moves from Adam to the Apocalypse. It includes six visions in Book 11 and six narratives in Book 12: altogether these cover three ages of world history – from Adam to Noah (in Book 11), from Noah to Christ, and from the apostles to the Second Coming. In the process, Adam is gradually educated in the history of human tribulation and salvation: he learns the movement of Christian history "From shadowy Types to Truth" (12.303), perceiving, as he watches and hears about the just few who will struggle in a world perverse, that there is a typological pattern which may be discerned with the inward eye of faith.

One thing that is adjusted crucially after the Fall is the relation of Adam and Eve to God. Adam fears that he will be deprived of the "Presence Divine" (11.315ff.), the kind of personal intimacy between man and God (with his "bright appearances") that Milton dramatized in Book 8 or that George Herbert recalls in his poem "Decay": "one might have sought and found thee presently / At some fair oak, or bush, or cave, or well." But Michael explains that in future history there will be a new kind of presence in the midst of absence. God will manifest his presence in "many a sign / Still following thee" (11.351–2) and further revealed in those "written Records pure"; signs and symbols may declare God's absence in history, but if interpreted rightly they also affirm his ongoing presence. Now Adam will "walk / As in his presence, ever to observe / His providence" (12.562–4): so Adam understands by the end of Book 12 the new relation that exists between man as exile and God. But understanding that new presence in absence in future history involves an ongoing process of interpreting signs, symbols, "types / And shadows" (12.232–3). Consequently, Michael's prophecy engages Adam, through dialogue and dramatic exchange with his angelic teacher, in the challenging process of actively learning how to read the emblematic visions and narratives of history (which, indeed, at times he misconstrues, as in the case of the vision of Jubal and Tubalcain and that world of fallen eroticism: see 11.598–602).

Death, Adam learns from Michael, will have many shapes – first by murder (in the vision of Cain and Abel) and then (in the Lazar house vision) by diseases of the body and mind:

> Daemoniac Frenzy, moping Melancholy
> And Moon-struck madness, pining Atrophy,
> Marasmus, and wide-wasting Pestilence.   (11.485–7)

Milton added these lines to the second edition of *Paradise Lost*: the diseases of the mind are not differentiated in this vision (477ff.) from those of the body. Milton's desire to heal the mind – body duality finds perverse expression in this vision where the two are conjoined in the horrible catalogue of diseases. In such a fallen world, a "triumphant Death" will be a tyrannical presence, exulting like a victorious warrior as he shakes his dart. Suicide, however, is no proper Christian response to the tribulations of history: unlike the stoic Horatio in *Hamlet*, for whom suicide is a proper response to this harsh world (he is more "an antique Roman than a Dane"), Adam must "patiently attend / [His] dissolution" (11.551–2), a key qualification Milton added to the poem's second edition.

Michael's harrowing visions impress upon Adam the turbulence of human history characterized by "sharp tribulation" (11.63) and by conflict between the "unjust" and the "just." Abel is the first hero of faith mentioned by St. Paul in his Epistle to the Hebrews (ch. 11): Enoch, Noah, Abraham, Moses, and others are mentioned by Paul and figure prominently in Milton's panorama of history. Milton is fascinated by the "Just Man" immersed in an historical drama of conflict and yet nevertheless daring, like Enoch or Abdiel, to speak the "odious Truth" (11.704) while "fearless of reproach and scorn" (811). In the case of Enoch, the conflict erupts when the Biblical prophet finds himself in the midst of a world of Homeric violence and ambition:

> For in those days Might only shall be admir'd,
> And Valor and Heroic Virtue call'd;
> To overcome in Battle, and subdue
> Nations, and bring home spoils with infinite
> Man-slaughter . . .   (11.689ff.)

Those prophets in history are zealous and vehement figures who, like Jeremiah in Milton's *Reason of Church-Government*, dare to use "sharp, but saving words" (YP 1:804) as these social activists speak of "Right and Wrong, / Of Justice, of Religion" (11.666–7), though as the case of Enoch reveals, they may well not be successful in renovating society. Even Noah's efforts are "all in vain" (726), suggesting the uncertainty of human agency in altering the dark course of postlapsarian history.

Noah preaches conversion and repentance in a sybaritic age, a time of "luxury and riot, feast and dance," "pomp" and "Palaces" (11.715, 748, 750), a vision which recalls Milton's prose polemics against "these enormous riots of ungodly misrule that Prelaty hath wrought" in church and state (*Church-Government*, YP 1:861) or against "royalist excess and folly" (*Second Defense*, YP 4:681); even as late as *The Readie and Easie Way* (1660) Milton dared to warn his people against choosing a king "with a dissolute and haughtie court about him, of vast expence and luxurie, masks and revels" (YP 7:425). And so Michael's vision of misrule, pomp, luxury, and palaces also evokes a sybaritic Restoration milieu, a time of decadent earthly kingdoms, reminding us of the "Sons of Belial," and "the noise / Of riot" described in the epic catalogue of fallen angels in Book 1 (lines 490ff.). In such a "dark Age," when "all shall turn degenerate," others "cool'd in zeal" will "practice how to live secure" (11.801ff.), recalling the polemical Milton's deploring of "lukewarmnesse" among his own countrymen during the 1640s and 1650s and his preference instead for "lively zeale" and political activism (*An Apology*, YP 1:868–9).

The flood brings about the destruction of the mount of Paradise itself, a poignant passage when we recall the lushness and artifice of Paradise vividly created by the poet in Book 4: "A Silvan Scene, and as the ranks ascend / Shade above shade, a woody Theatre / Of stateliest view" (140–2). So the flood destroys such theatrical environs, its lushness stripped away in this moment of iconoclasm as it takes root in the Persian Gulf as "an Island salt and bare" (11.834). The destruction is nevertheless an important step in Adam's appreciation of the symbolic inner paradise, for he must learn that "God attributes to place / No sanctity" (836–7) and must no longer mourn the loss of Paradise as he radically readjusts his sense of place and divine presence. The concluding vision of the rainbow underscores God's new covenant and relation to mankind: the sign of the rainbow in heaven appearing with its "color'd streaks" and "as a flowery verge" (11.879, 881) recalls the faded garland in Book 9 (982ff.), here a symbol of redemption to be interpreted by Adam with the help of his divine instructor.

Michael's shift from visions to narratives in Book 12 (and away from visual representation) emphasizes the increasingly inward turn of this Protestant poem, while dramatizing the Pauline notion that "Faith cometh by hearing" the Word (Romans 10:17). Nevertheless, the angel will urge Adam to "behold" (12.142) and "See"

(162) what he describes, as Adam learns to perceive the historical patterns, types, and configurations with an interior prophetic vision. The first narrative describes the reign of the ambitious and spiteful Nimrod, the primal and archetypal tyrant in human history whose name means "rebel" and who disparages "fair equality" (12.26): a version of Satan and Antichrist, Nimrod is also the tyrannical politician Milton had represented in his political tracts, where he had explicitly compared Charles I to Nimrod, the builder of "that spiritual *Babel*" (YP 3:598) against whom the Puritan saints must wage their fierce apocalyptic struggle. Adam's impassioned response, moreover, expresses his instinctive republican values, which accord with Milton's antimonarchical polemics defending the liberty and rights of "free born Men" who are free to make their own laws without the constraint of an arbitrary power (YP 3:206, 573):

> O execrable Son so to aspire
> Above his Brethren, to himself assuming
> Authority usurpt, from God not giv'n . . .   (12.64ff.)

Praising Adam's response to his narrative, Michael explains the nature of inward tyranny as "upstart Passions" overthrow "right Reason," recalling the effects after the Fall when "sensual Appetite" usurped "sovran Reason" (9.1129–30), leading to Adam and Eve's inward chaos. Here in Book 12 we can still hear the voice of the politically engaged Milton – the polemicist who blasted tyranny in his prose tracts dares to do it again after the Restoration in the more universal context of his sacred epic.

The narrative of Abraham, another figure of faith, enables Adam to perceive the typological drama of history with his inward eye of faith, since "by that Seed / Is meant thy great deliverer, who shall bruise / The Serpent's head" (12.148–50). And Moses, himself a prototype of the Protestant "Saint" wielding God's "wondrous power" (12.200), fights an apocalyptic battle against the rageful Pharaoh who, with "his stubborn heart" (193) and lawless tyranny, resembles Antichrist, Satan, or even a Stuart tyrant. But as Adam learns in the narrative of Moses, the law of Moses itself is only a type (as Milton argued in his *Christian Doctrine*) – a law to be superseded by a law of faith written in the hearts of individual believers. And so Michael, countering law with gospel, shows how the rhythm of Christian history moves "From shadowy Types to Truth . . . / From imposition of strict Laws, to free / Acceptance of large Grace" (12.303–5). Moreover, insofar as a fight between the forces of Antichrist and Christ continues in history, it will do so inwardly – "In thee and in thy Seed," Michael tells Adam, not as an epic-style "Duel" (12.395, 387), the kind he heard about in Raphael's narrative of the war in Heaven. The distinction between external and interior warfare again underscores the crucial distinction between classical heroic values and the intensely inward vision of Milton's Protestant poem.

Paradise Lost, we have seen, by no means suggests that the Fall was fortunate: as God says to Michael, "Happier, had it suffic'd [Man] to have known / Good by itself, and Evil not at all" (11.88–9). And yet after Adam hears from Michael about the Last Judgement, he bursts into his celebration of the famous *felix culpa*:

> O goodness infinite, goodness immense!
> That all this good out of evil shall produce,
> And evil turn to good . . .   (12.469ff.)

This celebration of the paradoxes of Christian history, however, is placed in a dark context, which qualifies its force: the narrative of history turns grim as Michael recounts what will happen after the time of the apostles who lived by the inward spirit and the law of faith. The passage beginning at line 508 ("Wolves shall succeed for teachers, grievous Wolves . . .") is indeed the darkest in the poem. Here, Michael relates the failure of ecclesiastical reformation all the way until the post-Restoration period of Milton's age. The image of Truth in a world perverse retiring "Bestuck with sland'rous darts" recalls the famous image of "the torn body of our martyr'd Saint" Truth in *Areopagitica* (YP 2:549–50): in *Paradise Lost* Milton is cursing faithless and superstitious periods when religion is satisfied only by "outward Rites and specious forms." There is nevertheless a note of defiance in this dark prophecy of "heavy persecution": Milton's condemnation of "Secular power" and of the forcing of consciences is as firm as it ever was in his pre-Restoration tracts. The apocalyptic promise of "New Heav'ns, new Earth" (547–51), which counters this sorrowful depiction of history, offers some hope but cannot fully offset the bleakness of the preceding lines; simply too much narrative weight is given in Michael's prophecy to the historical pattern of decline. Indeed, the conflicting historical patterns at the end of *Paradise Lost*, powerful as they are, offer little sense of triumphant emotional and aesthetic resolution.

Despite what has often been a haunting account of the future, Adam does experience at the end something like "calm of mind," all passion having been spent (to quote the end of *Samson Agonistes*); if knowledge is as food, Adam has had his fill and is now ready to depart: "Greatly instructed I shall hence depart, / Greatly in peace of thought, and have my fill / Of knowledge" (12.557–9). Adam has learned two crucial lessons: about the symbolic nature of divine presence and about how weakness may also manifest an unresistable might. Milton's great poems, including *Samson* and *Paradise Regained*, dramatize how it is possible to accomplish "great things" "by small," how by "things deem'd weak" it is possible to subvert the "worldly strong," and about how the "simply meek" may indeed overcome the "worldly wise" (12.566–9), recalling one of Milton's favorite scriptural passages, 2 Corinthians 12:9. Having well learned his historical lessons, through a series of challenging and trying visions and narratives, Adam now becomes, in effect, the first Christian: "Taught this by his example whom I now / Acknowledge my Redeemer ever blest" (12.572–3). At the beginning of his poem, Milton announces the central themes of disobedience and loss; yet he also reminds us of the restoration brought by "one greater Man."

Adam and Eve may now possess "A paradise within" them, "happier far" (12.587) – happier, that is, than the destruction of postlapsarian Eden which they leave behind, though not happier, it should be stressed, than the rich and various prelapsarian life they have lost and which Milton had described so fully earlier in the poem. Paradise at the end of Milton's visionary epic is not so much a place as a symbol, located within the heart of the individual Protestant exile and believer. The true believer may carry the paradise within, just as Satan carries Hell within him, whichever way he flies. Symbolic of our crime and expulsion, the inner paradise is symbolic as well of the possibility for internal renewal in the face of the crises and trials of human history which Adam has just learned about.

Much of the vision of history in the last two books does indeed seem unsettling, its historical characters often "acting little more than mute persons in a Scene" (to borrow words from Milton's *History of Britain*). But the poem does conclude on a more generous note – one that mollifies the harshness of its historical visions and narratives. Not only has Adam learned to make a strength of his weakness, but Eve – to whom Milton significantly gives the last prophetic speech in *Paradise Lost* – concludes by underscoring her role in history as agent of both destruction and restoration:

> though all by mee is lost,
> Such favor I unworthy am voutsaf't,
> By mee the Promis'd Seed shall all restore.   (12.621–3)

This is "*our* Mother" (12.624; emphasis added) who speaks here and who is given that crucial word "restore" balanced against that key word "lost." By the end of the poem, we have made peace with our fallen parents and are meant to identify fully with them, as the narrator himself had done at the very end of Book 10, where his concluding lines echo the words of the contrite Adam. We see our first parents "ling'ring" (12.638) – the adjective registers perfectly their hesitation at leaving behind their former "happy seat" which they do with "wand'ring steps and slow" – as they are about to become georgic laborers in the fallen world.

Moreover, as the poem's final evocative and open-ended lines suggest, postlapsarian history still contains for humankind possibility, choice, and individual responsibility, even in a fallen world where, as Adam and Eve now well know, their children will encounter periods of great political upheaval and religious persecution. The emphasis here, at the end of *Paradise Lost*, is on their choosing, on what they can make for themselves in fallen history, as they are given "many a sign" (11.351) of God's providence:

> The World was all before them, where to choose
> Thir place of rest, and Providence thir guide:
> They hand in hand with wand'ring steps and slow,
> Through *Eden* took thir solitary way.

Milton's lines allude to Psalm 107: "They wandered in the wilderness in a solitary way . . . Then they cried unto the Lord in their trouble, *and* he delivered them out of their distresses." Milton began his great poem with Satan and his demons; and so he ends it, quietly and movingly, with our mother and father, its human actors. In Book 9, we saw Eve ominously withdraw her hand from Adam's: now we see them walk "hand and hand" once more, the first couple united in exile as they leave Eden with divine promise in order to face an uncertain future and a new beginning.

Chapter 3

The literary after-life of *Paradise Lost*

20 Revisions from the Restoration to the Romantics

Highly ambitious for himself, the younger Milton hoped to produce a great poem "so written to aftertimes, as they should not willingly let it die" (YP 1:810). *Paradise Lost* – in many ways the greatest and last of the English epics – had a profound effect on subsequent literary history. Its rich and complex influence is too vast a subject to distill within a short account, but a brief look at the ways selected writers from the Restoration to the Romantic period revised or reworked Milton's poem can show how it continued to live on and serve as a powerful creative stimulus.

We can begin with Milton's own "brief epic" *Paradise Regained* (1671), a four-book poem again focused on the drama of temptation – Satan's spectacular temptations of Jesus in the wilderness (the chief biblical source is Luke 4:1–13). This intensely inward poem about the triumphs of the second Adam over his guileful adversary, however, lacks much of the epic machinery of *Paradise Lost*. Milton's Jesus is unknown, contemplative, private and poor – hardly the traditional aristocratic epic hero who defines himself by great acts of martial prowess. Moreover, the solitary Jesus can express uncertainty ("Where will this end?," 2.245) as he proceeds to unravel the meaning of his prophetic vocation as Messiah. And yet Jesus's "deeds" are "Above Heroic" (1.14–15): in his spiritual warfare with Satan, he exemplifies yet once more how mighty weakness can overcome "Satanic strength" (1.161). One temptation, a luxurious banquet offered to the hungry Jesus, explicitly recalls *Paradise Lost*: "Alas how simple, to these Cates compar'd / Was that crude Apple that diverted *Eve!*" (2.348–9), Milton observes. Jesus remains unmoved by this regal feast, resisting the temptation to which the first Adam and Eve succumbed. Indeed, Milton's "one greater Man" encounters sensual, active, and intellectual temptations – a poetic scheme of total temptation – and rejects them all. The lure of riches, martial glory, revolutionary action, imperial power, and Greek learning and arts will not alter his resolve. In a poem where the duelling is verbal rather than martial, Milton's inward-looking Jesus is increasingly fervent in his responses to that rhetoric that "won so much on *Eve*" (4.5). Basing his prophetic authority on "*Sion's* songs" (4.347), Jesus is victorious at the end of *Paradise Regained*: his small actions prove to be truly apocalyptic as they foreshadow his final battle with and victory over Satan. Milton's poetic sequel to *Paradise Lost* dramatizes how the second Adam, manifesting perfect obedience in the midst of the wilderness of this world, "hast aveng'd / Supplanted *Adam*," "regain'd lost Paradise," and overcome the "Infernal Serpent" (4.606–8, 618).

It was not until its lavish fourth edition (1688), illustrated by John Baptist de Medina, however, that *Paradise Lost* began to stimulate many new editions, widespread commentary, and extensive annotations. Yet in the year its second edition appeared (1674), it was already regarded as a vernacular classic by one of the Restoration's chief literary figures. That year Milton's younger contemporary, the Poet Laureate Dryden, wrote *The State of Innocence and the Fall of Man*, a rhymed, unstaged operatic version of Milton's poem that condenses its more than 10,000 lines into five acts. Dryden recognized Milton's genius, calling *Paradise Lost* "one of the greatest, most noble, and most sublime POEMS, which either this Age or Nation has produc'd" (*Dramatic Works*, ed. M. Summers [1932], III, p. 417); England had produced an epic that matched the achievements of the ancients. But in rewriting *Paradise Lost* as drama, the form Milton himself originally considered, Dryden reduced the cosmic and heroic scope of the epic. In Dryden's adaptation, we never see the Father and Son or Sin and Death; and Dryden omits altogether Satan's daring journey through Chaos, the war in Heaven, the Creation, and Christ's sacrifice for mankind. Dryden's Lucifer conveys little of the heroic defiance of Milton's Satan: thus in Dryden's version, Satan's forceful assertion that it is "Better to reign in Hell, than serve in Heav'n" (*PL* 1.263) is uttered by Moloch not Lucifer. Instead, Dryden emphasizes the domestic drama between Adam and Eve (sometimes rendered in the stylized language and worldly idiom of Restoration comedy), along with the temptation, Fall, and reconciliation. He reduces the poem's sad vision of future ages and mentions only briefly the "paradise within"; his work, moreover, ends on a strongly optimistic note as Adam and Eve depart in peace. His remarkably compact Restoration version does engage some of the challenging theological issues of *Paradise Lost*, including human free will and divine pre-destination (which Adam debates with two angels in Act IV), but overall it diminishes the visionary and inward dimensions of Milton's prophetic poem.

Dryden never fulfilled his own ambition to write an epic; still, *Paradise Lost* influenced his finest heroic satire. Full of Miltonic allusions and language, his political poem *Absalom and Achitophel* (1681) casts the earl of Shaftesbury (Achitophel) in the role of the Miltonic Satan who has fallen from greatness and possesses "A fiery Soul" (156), while presenting the youthful and handsome duke of Monmouth (Absalom) as the tempted Adam who rebels against his father, Charles II ("the Godlike *David*," 1030), and attempts to replace James, duke of York, as heir to the throne. The king's defiant enemies in the poem resemble Milton's rebel angels in Hell: "Some had in Courts been Great, and thrown from thence, / Like Fiends, were harden'd in Impenitence" (144–5). Although Dryden employs Old Testament analogies in his brilliant satire against Shaftesbury's Whig party, he, unlike Milton, is not especially concerned with theological questions. Dryden's focus is the volatile and complex partisan world of Restoration politics: seducing a pliable Absalom "with studied Arts" (228), his Satanic Shaftesbury – an immensely talented but scheming politician and rhetorician – is engaged in a pernicious conspiracy "to Ruine Church and State" (930) and undermine the lawful king. Aligning himself with the king's cause, the Restoration Dryden supported political and religious beliefs remote from those of the radical Puritan who wrote *Paradise Lost*; nevertheless, he was able to appropriate skillfully the epic situation, tone, and language of Milton's poem for his own purposes – to address in an imaginative mode a major political crisis of his time.

Like Dryden, Pope aspired to write a national epic – one on the subject of Brutus, a project Milton himself considered and Pope never completed. Instead, writing in an age uneasy with the heroic values of martial epic, Pope excelled at the mock-epic, a form partly stimulated by *Paradise Lost*, which uses the mock-heroic to ridicule Satan. In *The Rape of the Lock* (1712–14), Pope brilliantly uses the grand epic style for a trivial subject: the severed lock of Arabella Fermor provided the occasion for a poem sometimes seen as an amusing rewriting of Milton's myth of the Fall. The charming Belinda, the poem's Eve figure, gazes at her "heav'nly Image" (1.125) in a mirror, is vulnerable to pride, and suffers a fall at the hands of a Baron who will use "Fraud or Force" (2.34) to attain his ends. Yet despite its playful Miltonic allusions (e.g. its supernatural sylphs parody Milton's guardian angels), the poem's dazzling world of social artifice seems far removed from Milton's baroque cosmos where the spirit world is indeed real and where the forces of good and evil struggle mightily. A more significant reworking of Miltonic myths occurs in Pope's *Dunciad* (published in four books in 1743): this sprawling, exuberant satire on the triumph of mindless dullness, hack writing, and pedantry, concludes with an apocalyptic vision of the collapse of civilization. Pope depicts the "uncreating word" of the "Anarch" Chaos restoring "Universal Darkness" (4.654–6) – thus reversing the divine and human creative forces which animate the universe of *Paradise Lost*. Pope has transformed visionary Miltonic epic into visionary satire. His satiric epic reworks Miltonic materials often to comic effect: the goddess Dulness, daughter of Chaos and Night, engages in "wild creation" (1.82), a parody of God's creation in Milton's poem; and the King Dunce, based on the witless writer Colley Cibber, is a parodic version of both Satan (Cibber sits "High on a gorgeous seat," 2.1) and the Son of God since he possesses Dulness' "Image full exprest" (1.107). Moreover, the dunces' London is a satiric version of Milton's Hell: their epic contest of noise in Book 2 recalls "the wild uproar" generated by the devils' underworld activities, as well as Milton's noisy Chaos. Even Pope's petition for "one dim Ray of Light" (4.1) in an encroaching world of darkness is a witty revision of Milton's invocation to Holy Light.

The Edenic myth of *Paradise Lost* stimulated eighteenth-century poets in other ways. In Pope's topographical *Windsor Forest* (1713), "The Groves of *Eden*" which "look green in Song" are set in the prosperous and peaceful Stuart England of Queen Anne: Pope rewrites Milton's myth of Eden, giving his reader a guided tour through a carefully arranged landscape of balanced antitheses signifying "Order in Variety" (see lines 7–42). For Pope, Milton's earthly paradise is not lost but survives (however precariously) and can be reimagined – made to live again through Pope's artifice, while given fresh political and historical symbolism in the context of the British empire and the Peace of Utrecht, which the poem celebrates. Pope's acquaintance, Anne Finch, countess of Winchilsea, responded differently to Milton's myth of Eden. In her fine Miltonic poem, "The Petition for an Absolute Retreat" (1713), she reimagines the myth from the perspective of Eve: Finch dreams of regaining Paradise, a secure rural retreat where fallen passions are banished and where she enjoys the pleasures of solitude, a feast of fruits managed without her care, a wise and witty female friend, and "A *Partner* suited to [her] Mind."

Milton's prophetic poem had a profound and complex effect on the Romantic literary imagination. Blake wrote a long prophetic and mythological poem entitled *Milton* (1804–8) intended "To Justify the Ways of God to Men," a theodicy that addresses the problem of evil in Blake's day and that presents the radical Milton as a bard of visionary emancipation and art. Milton descends from heaven, struggles with Urizen (the circumscriber of the fallen world), reincarnates himself in Blake, and heroically redeems a fallen Albion (England). Inspired by Old Testament prophecies and apocalyptic visions, Blake saw himself as a mythmaking poet in the line of the revolutionary Milton whom he both admired and criticized. His most memorable response to *Paradise Lost* occurs in *The Marriage of Heaven and Hell* (1790–3), where he notes that "The reason Milton wrote in fetters when he wrote of Angels & God, and at liberty when of Devils & Hell, is because he was a true Poet and of the Devils party without knowing it." Blake's provocative point is that unconsciously Milton was on the side not of the rational God and Messiah but on the side of Satan – that is, the forces of energy, imagination, excess, and unrestrained desire which institutional Christianity represses. According to Blake, visionary poetry derives from energy: Milton's imaginative powers are therefore most evident in the scenes in Hell. In *A Defence of Poetry* (1821), Shelley too admired the energy, as well as the perseverance, of Milton's Satan, seeing him as "a moral being" "far superior" to Milton's God who inflicts "the most horrible revenge upon his enemy." Yet Shelley was by no means an unqualified Satanist, for he could acknowledge the pernicious side of Satan's implacable hatred and anarchic will – "the taints of ambition, envy, revenge, and desire for personal aggrandizement" (Preface to *Prometheus Unbound* [1819]) – which make him an imperfect Prometheus, a Titanic rebel whose courage is vitiated by his vindictiveness.

Keats likewise responded imaginatively to *Paradise Lost*, which he studied intensely during the winter of 1817–18. Some of his famous statements do indeed seem to confirm Harold Bloom's claim in *The Anxiety of Influence* (1973) that Romantic poets struggled anxiously with the formidable achievements of Milton, their great precursor whose inhibiting influence they tried to resist: "Life to him would be death to me," Keats writes of Milton in one letter (September 24, 1819), and in another he admits that he has abandoned *The Fall of Hyperion* (1819), which followed his earlier Miltonic *Hyperion*, because "there were too many Miltonic inversions in it" (September 21, 1819). But Keats also observed, as he was working on *The Fall of Hyperion*, that "fine writing is next to fine doing the top thing in the world" and that "Paradise Lost becomes a greater wonder" to him (August 24, 1819) – a powerful source of poetic recreation. The opening setting of *The Fall*'s allegorical dream vision recalls Milton's pastoral paradise and Eve's Edenic meal: having satisfied his "appetite" on the remains of this Miltonic feast – thereby giving him a taste of lost innocence – the poet falls into a swoon and dreams. The dream itself concerns his education in tragic knowledge and suffering. As he ascends with difficulty the steps of a somber temple, we are reminded of Adam's ascent up the hill of vision in Book 11. Reworking the dramatic exchanges between Michael and Adam, Keats portrays the poet-dreamer's interchange with the stern and sorrowful prophetess, Moneta, who removes his mind's "film," tests him, and shows him the misery of the fallen Saturn and the goddess Thea. Keats's allegorical recreation of *Paradise Lost* thus enables him to explore the struggles the genuine poet must undergo and the tragic vision he must acquire.

Wordsworth himself regarded Milton's visionary epic as among "the grand store-houses of enthusiastic and meditative Imagination" (1815 Preface to *The Lyrical Ballads*). A creative and original revision of *Paradise Lost*, Wordsworth's *Prelude* (1805; 1850) is an epic-scale poem which traces and analyzes the development of the Romantic poet's mind from his earliest years to his maturity. His interiorized epic of the self (the poet Coleridge is its Muse) begins where Milton's great poem ends:

> The earth is all before me – with a heart
> Joyous, nor scared at its own liberty,
> I look about, and should the guide I chuse
> Be nothing better than a wandering cloud,
> I cannot miss my way.   (1805 *Prelude*, Book 1.15–19)

Whereas Milton ends with the expulsion of Adam and Eve from Paradise, Wordsworth – feeling a sense of renewal as he leaves the fallen world of the city – begins by referring to the regaining of Paradise through the "gentle breeze" (1) without and the "corresponding mild creative breeze" (43) within, his spontaneous imaginative powers and energy. No less than Milton, Wordsworth writes as a poet-prophet who sees himself as chosen in his sacred vocation; he hopes, moreover, to equal and transform the ambitious epic achievement of his visionary predecessor. Thus he writes as a prophet of Nature who explores the dynamic interaction between the sublime natural world, with its combination of majesty and awesomeness, and the power of his poetic imagination. For Wordsworth, Providence refers to natural objects which guide him in his wanderings through time. Indeed, whereas *Paradise Lost* creates its mythology from the older materials of the classical world and the Bible, *The Prelude* creates its mythology and "heroic argument" (3.182) out of Wordsworth's own personal and subjective experiences. As he reflects on his intense childhood experiences in the Lake District, his school years, his hopes for and disappointment in the French Revolution, his discontented life in the city, and his epiphanic moments in Nature, the Romantic poet rewrites Milton's mythic story of Edenic innocence followed by the Fall and redemption – Wordsworth's regaining of a higher innocence through his powers of imagination and memory.

Among the more remarkable Romantic texts, Mary Shelley's powerful gothic novel *Frankenstein, or the Modern Prometheus* (1818) owes much of its inspiration to Milton's *Paradise Lost*. Hideous in appearance and supernatural in size and strength, the tragic monster created and abandoned by the scientist Frankenstein comes to perceive his miserable identity and alienated condition through his emotional reading of Milton's poem "as a true history" (ch. 15). Like Milton's Adam, the solitary monster intensely yearns for an Eve, a female counter-part of his own hideous kind; and like the fallen Adam he is expelled by his maker "with all the world before [him]" (ch. 16), though without Providence as his guide. Yet he also painfully recognizes striking differences between himself and Adam: Adam at first was "a perfect creature, happy and prosperous, guarded by the special care of his Creator . . . but I was wretched, helpless, and alone" (ch. 15). Feeling not only a profound sense of anguish, but a passion for revenge after being rejected by his creator and mankind, the daemon perceives his closer affinity with the fallen Satan in his antagonism towards God. "Evil thenceforth became my good" (ch. 24), he observes, echoing Satan's resolve at the end of his first soliloquy – "Evil be thou my Good" (4.110). Indeed, this monster's acute sense of Hell and its torments is no less internalized than Satan's: "I, like the archfiend, bore a hell within me" (ch. 16). The monster is more benevolent than his Miltonic counterpart, but his feelings of rage against his creator – whom he sees as a heartless tormenter – recall the hatred of Satan for his maker, fuelled by his exclusion from bliss: "Remember, that I am thy creature," says the monster, "I ought to be thy Adam; but I am rather the fallen angel, whom thou drivest from joy for no misdeed" (ch. 10). Taking its epigraph from the fallen Adam's dark complaint in Book 10 against God ("Did I request thee, Maker, from my Clay to mould me Man . . .?"), Mary Shelley's secular myth of the modern Prometheus raises disturbing questions about the godlike creator who violates nature, who neglects to take responsibility for his creation, and who never adequately justifies his ways. Shattered at the end, Frankenstein sees himself as "the archangel who aspired to omnipotence" but is now "chained in an eternal hell" (ch. 24). As the Faustian aspirer who suffers a great fall, the Romantic creator has himself become another version of the Miltonic Satan.

Guide to further reading

Because the volume of scholarship on *Paradise Lost* is so vast, I have chosen to highlight book-length works, including important collections of essays. For articles on Milton, readers may wish to consult *Milton Quarterly* (1967–) and the annual volumes in *Milton Studies* (Pittsburgh, 1969–).

Bibliographies and reference works

For Milton scholarship the following bibliographies are useful: Calvin Huckabay, *John Milton: An Annotated Bibliography, 1929–1968*, rev. edn (Pittsburgh, 1969); James H. Hanford and William McQueen, *Milton*, 2nd edn (Arlington Heights, IL, 1979); C. A. Patrides, *An Annotated Critical Bibliography of John Milton* (New York, 1987); P. J. Klemp, *The Essential Milton: An Annotated Bibliography of Major Modern Studies* (Boston, MA, 1989); P. J. Klemp, *Paradise Lost: An Annotated Bibliography* (Lanham, MD, and London, 1996). James H. Hanford and James G. Taffe, *A Milton Handbook*, 5th edn (New York, 1970), is a valuable reference work on the poet and his writings, as is *A Milton Encyclopedia*, gen. ed. William B. Hunter, 9 vols. (Lewisburg, PA, 1978–83). Currently in preparation is the *Yale Milton Encyclopedia*, ed. Thomas N. Corns, with a projected publication date of 2005.

Editions

Milton: Complete Poetry and Selected Prose, ed. Merritt Y. Hughes (Indianapolis, 1957), widely used in the USA, combines modernization of Milton's spelling and punctuation, while preserving "conspicuous seventeenth-century typographical peculiarities." The most precise, helpful, and extensive scholarly notes on *Paradise Lost*, however, can be found in *Milton: Paradise Lost*, ed. Alastair Fowler (London, 1971; 2nd edn, 1998), first published in *The Poems of John Milton*, ed. John Carey and Fowler (1968); Fowler's edition modernizes spelling but not punctuation. *Paradise Lost*, ed. Scott Elledge (New York, 1975) includes useful annotations, as well as background and critical materials; *John Milton: Paradise Lost*, ed. John Leonard (Harmondsworth, 2000) contains concise and exact notes, which are particularly valuable for readers approaching the poem for the first time. Other accessible modernized and annotated editions of Milton include *John Milton: Complete English Poems, Of Education, Areopagitica*, ed. Gordon Campbell, 4th edn (London, 1993) and *John Milton*, ed. Stephen Orgel and Jonathan Goldberg (Oxford, 1990). *The Riverside Milton*, ed. Roy Flannagan (Boston and New York, 1998), which retains original spelling and punctuation, includes copious annotations on *Paradise Lost*.

Biography

For the earliest biographies, including those by Milton's contemporaries, see *The Early Lives of Milton*, ed. Helen Darbishire (London, 1932). J. H. Hanford, *John Milton, Englishman* (New York, 1949), remains a good, readable biography. Lively but less reliable is A. N. Wilson, *The Life of John Milton* (Oxford, 1983). The standard scholarly biography is William R. Parker, *Milton: A Biography*, 2 vols. (Oxford, 1968; 2nd edn revised by Gordon Campbell, 1996). John Diekhoff, *Milton on Himself* (Oxford, 1939; rev. edn, 1965), collects Milton's many statements about himself and his works. The best critical biography, providing rich treatments of Milton's writings in their cultural and reformist contexts, is now Barbara K. Lewalski, *The Life of John Milton* (Oxford, 2000). Readers who prefer a shorter account of Milton's life and works may turn to Cedric C. Brown, *John Milton: A Literary Life* (New York, 1995). The poet's early education is examined by Donald L. Clark, *Milton at St. Paul's School* (New York, 1948). J. Milton French has compiled essential information pertaining to Milton in *The Life Records of John Milton*, 5 vols. (New Brunswick, 1949–58), as has Gordon Campbell in *A Milton Chronology* (London and New York, 1997), which supplements French with fresh biographical material. There is also a good deal of biographical material in Christopher Hill's *Milton and the English Revolution* (see below). Finally, the great Victorian biography by David Masson, *The Life of John Milton* 7 vols. (London, 1859–94), remains a valuable resource for students of Milton and his age.

Cultural and historical context

For good introductions to Milton's cultural and historical contexts, the reader may consult the following books: *The Cambridge Companion to Milton*, ed. Dennis Danielson (Cambridge, 1989; 2nd edn, 1999) serves as a helpful guide to Milton's *oeuvre*, while the richest and fullest guide to Milton's cultural, political, and religious contexts can now be found in *A Companion to Milton*, ed. Thomas N. Corns (Oxford, 2001). *The Age of Milton: Backgrounds to Seventeenth-Century Literature*, ed. C. A. Patrides and R. B. Waddington (Manchester, 1980), contains helpful essays on the poet's cultural, social, and historical contexts; it also includes useful lists of primary and secondary sources.

A particularly rich study of Milton's historical context is Christopher Hill's *Milton and the English Revolution* (London, 1977), which examines the poet's great poems in terms of his radical milieu. In *The Experience of Defeat: Milton and Some Contemporaries* (London, 1984), Hill considers the poet's responses to the defeat of the English Revolution. An important study of nonconformity in the period, with particular relevance for Milton, is N. H. Keeble, *The Literary Culture of Nonconformity in Later Seventeenth-Century England* (Leicester and Athens, GA, 1987). An increasing number of studies have attempted to illuminate, from various perspectives, the politics of *Paradise Lost* in terms of the political and religious conflicts of the revolutionary years and the Restoration: these include Stevie Davies, *Images of Kingship in Paradise Lost: Milton's Politics and Christian Liberty* (Columbia, MO, 1983); Sharon Achinstein, *Milton and the Revolutionary Reader* (Princeton, 1994); Laura L. Knoppers, *Historicizing Milton: Spectacle, Power, and Poetry in Restoration England* (Athens, GA, and London, 1994); Robert T. Fallon, *Divided Empire: Milton's Political Imagery* (University Park, PA, 1995); John N. King, *Milton and Religious Controversy* (Cambridge, 2000); and David Loewenstein, *Representing Revolution in Milton and his Contemporaries: Religion, Politics, and Polemics in Radical Puritanism* (Cambridge, 2001). The most notable attempt to situate the poem in a republican context is David Norbrook, *Writing the English Republic* (Cambridge, 1999).

On the philosophical materialism or monism of *Paradise Lost* in the context of Milton's age, readers will find Stephen Fallon's *Milton among the Philosophers* (Ithaca, NY, 1991) especially illuminating. On the poem in relation to science, see Walter C. Curry, *Milton's Ontology, Cosmogony and Physics* (Lexington, 1957); Kester Svendsen, *Milton and Science* (Cambridge, MA, 1956); Harinder Singh Marjara, *Contemplation of Created Things: Science in Paradise Lost* (Toronto, 1992); and William Kerrigan's *Sacred Complex* (see below). Karen L. Edwards, *Milton and the Natural World: Science and Poetry in Paradise Lost* (Cambridge, 1999) examines the poem's relation to seventeenth-century natural history and persuasively challenges the orthodox view, represented by Svendsen, that the poem is a monument to the old science. The relation between science and politics in *Paradise Lost* is explored well in John Rogers, *The Matter of Revolution: Science, Poetry, and Politics in the Age of Milton* (Ithaca, NY, 1996). Readers curious about the angelology of Milton's age can consult Robert West, *Milton and the Angels* (Athens, GA, 1955).

For readers who wish to gain an appreciation of *Paradise Lost* in relation to its contemporary analogues, see Watson Kirkconnell, *The Celestial Cycle* (Toronto, 1952), which provides translations of continental texts.

Other critical studies

The large number of critical studies devoted to *Paradise Lost* requires that I be highly selective here. For additional works, the reader may consult the bibliographies cited above, as well as Margarita Stocker, *Paradise Lost: An Introduction to the Variety of Criticism* (Atlantic Highlands, NJ, 1988). Among introductory studies, I would single out Joseph H. Summers, *The Muse's Method* (Cambridge, MA, 1962), an elegant and sensitive reading of the poem; G. K. Hunter's *Paradise Lost* (London, 1980) may also be consulted with profit. Thomas N. Corns, *Regaining Paradise Lost* (London and New York, 1994), is a perceptive introduction to the poem in its original cultural contexts. C. S. Lewis's *A Preface to Paradise Lost* (London, 1942) offers a lively account of the poem's epic features, though his alignment of Milton with Christian orthodoxy has rightly been questioned. John P. Rumrich's *Matter of Glory: A New Preface to Paradise Lost* (Pittsburgh, 1987), in contrast to Lewis, examines the poetic implications of Milton's heretical materialism. W. B. C. Watkins, *An Anatomy of Milton's Verse* (Baton Rouge, 1955), is a fine introduction to the sensuous and passionate elements of Milton's poetry. Readers interested in the development of Milton's poetic career may find the following helpful: E. M. W. Tillyard, *Milton*, rev. edn (London, 1966); J. H. Hanford, *John Milton: Poet and Humanist* (Cleveland, 1966); Louis L. Martz, *Poet of Exile: A Study of Milton's Poetry* (New Haven, 1980); Edward W. Tayler, *Milton's Poetry: Its Development in Time* (Pittsburgh, 1979).

One of the most illuminating discussions of *Paradise Lost*'s subversive relation to its epic precursors is Joan M. Webber's *Milton and His Epic Tradition* (Seattle, 1979). Thomas M. Greene's *The Descent from Heaven* (New Haven, 1963), a fine general study of epic, also includes a discriminating discussion of *Paradise Lost* in relation to its European predecessors, while David Quint's *Epic and Empire: Politics and Generic Form from Virgil to Milton* (Princeton, 1993) examines *Paradise Lost* in terms of its political topicality and its rejection of epic nationhood. Other useful studies include John M. Steadman, *Milton and the Renaissance Hero* (Oxford, 1967); Francis C. Blessington, *Paradise Lost and the Classical Epic* (London, 1979); Charles Martindale, *John Milton and the Transformation of Ancient Epic* (London, 1986); and Davis P. Harding, *The Club of Hercules: Studies in the Classical Background of Paradise*

Lost (Urbana, 1962). Martz's *Poet of Exile* discusses the influence of Ovid on Milton's poetry, as does Richard J. DuRocher, *Milton and Ovid* (Ithaca, NY, 1985). For studies of the classical epics which *Paradise Lost* revises, see the Landmarks books by Michael Silk on *The Iliad* (Cambridge, 1987; 2nd edn, 2004), Jasper Griffin on *The Odyssey* (Cambridge, 1987; 2nd edn, 2004), and K. W. Gransden on *The Aeneid* (Cambridge, 1990; 2nd edn, 2004). Supplementing studies of *Paradise Lost* in relation to classical, medieval, and Renaissance epic is J. Martin Evans' account of the poem in terms of seventeenth-century colonial discourse: *Milton's Imperial Epic: Paradise Lost and the Discourse of Colonialism* (Ithaca, NY, 1996). The fullest, most precise account of the poem's generic features is Barbara K. Lewalski's *Paradise Lost and the Rhetoric of Literary Forms* (Princeton, 1985).

Notable studies of the poem's style include Christopher Ricks, *Milton's Grand Style* (Oxford, 1963); Arnold Stein, *Answerable Style* (Minneapolis, 1953); and James Whaler, *Counterpoint and Symbol: An Inquiry into the Rhythm of Milton's Epic Style* (Copenhagen, 1956). On lexical and syntactic matters, Thomas N. Corns, *Milton's Language* (Oxford, 1990), is helpful. Readers wishing to sample earlier modern criticisms of Milton's style, which Ricks persuasively answered, may examine T. S. Eliot, "A Note on the Verse of John Milton" (1936) and "Milton" (1947), both reprinted in *On Poetry and Poets* (London, 1957); and three essays by F. R. Leavis in *Revaluation* (London, 1936) and *The Common Pursuit* (London, 1952). Ricks demonstrated the precision, subtlety, and complexity of Milton's style, whereas Eliot and Leavis had claimed it was mechanical, artificial, and remote from ordinary speech. Building on the work of Ricks, John Leonard's *Naming in Paradise: Milton and the Language of Adam and Eve* (Oxford, 1990) offers a sensitive analysis of pre- and postlapsarian language in the poem. For perceptive analyses of multilingual interactions in the style and language of *Paradise Lost*, see John K. Hale, *Milton's Languages* (Cambridge, 1997).

Focusing on the reader's unsettling experiences as the poem's subject, Stanley E. Fish's *Surprised by Sin: The Reader in Paradise Lost* (New York and London, 1967; 2nd edn, Cambridge, MA, 1997), remains one of the most stimulating books on *Paradise Lost*; B. Rajan's *Paradise Lost and the Seventeenth-Century Reader* (London, 1947) places more emphasis on Milton's contemporary readership. Valuable studies of the poet's prominent voice include Anne D. Ferry, *Milton's Epic Voice: The Narrator in Paradise Lost* (Cambridge, MA, 1963); William Riggs, *The Christian Poet in Paradise Lost* (Berkeley, 1972); and Arnold Stein, *The Art of Presence: The Poet and Paradise Lost* (Berkeley, 1977). On Milton's prophetic voice, see William Kerrigan's *Prophetic Milton* (Charlottesville, 1974), which examines Milton in relation to the complex history of prophecy. An important book stressing the poem's visionary dimensions but viewing Milton as sacerdotal is Michael Lieb's *Poetics of the Holy: A Reading of Paradise Lost* (Chapel Hill, 1981). Kerrigan's *Sacred Complex: On the Psychogenesis of Paradise Lost* (Cambridge, MA, 1983) is a powerful psychoanalytic study of the origins of the poet's creativity, as well as an illuminating account of the poem's religious symbolism.

Works addressing the theology of Milton's poem include Maurice Kelley's *This Great Argument* (Princeton, 1941), which stresses interconnections between the *Christian Doctrine* and the epic. Dennis Danielson's *Milton's Good God: A Study in Literary Theodicy* (Cambridge, 1982) valuably examines Milton's notion of free will in its seventeenth-century context. In contrast to Kelley, the technical studies by W. B. Hunter, C. A. Patrides, and J. H. Adamson in *Bright Essence: Studies in Milton's Theology* (Salt Lake City, 1973) tend to stress Milton's orthodoxy; however, the essays in *Milton and Heresy*, ed. Stephen B. Dobranski and John P. Rumrich (Cambridge, 1998), freshly illuminate the poet's heretical theology. For a polemical attack on Milton's authoritarian God, see William Empson, *Milton's God* (London, 1961), a brilliant but quirky book. While also critical of Milton's God in *Ruin the Sacred Truths: Poetry and Belief from the Bible to the Present* (Cambridge, MA, 1989), Harold Bloom is sympathetic to the poet's unorthodox and sensuous imagination. Notable studies of Milton's uses of the Bible include James H. Sims, *The Bible in Milton's Epics* (Gainsville, 1962), Regina M. Schwartz, *Remembering and Repeating: Biblical Creation in Paradise Lost* (Cambridge, 1988), and Dayton Haskin, *Milton's Burden of Interpretation* (Philadelphia, 1995), though indeed many studies cited in this guide inevitably touch on the topic. Dennis Burden, *The Logical Epic* (London, 1967), considers the rational elements of Milton's theodicy and narrative, while J. M. Evans, *Paradise Lost and the Genesis Tradition* (Oxford, 1968), examines Milton's original representation of the Edenic myth and the Fall in relation to traditional versions.

Of the many works treating issues of gender and sexuality in *Paradise Lost*, I particularly recommend James Grantham Turner's *One Flesh: Paradisal Marriage and Sexual Relations in the Age of Milton* (Oxford, 1987), a rich study of the multiple and contradictory interpretations of Genesis and sexuality that Milton confronted. Diane K. McColley's *Milton's Eve* (Urbana, 1983) argues for Eve's regenerative role in the poem; and *Milton and the Idea of Woman*, ed. Julia M. Walker (Urbana, 1988) examines Milton's representations of woman from a variety of critical perspectives.

Other studies of particular aspects of *Paradise Lost* include John R. Knott, *Milton's Pastoral Vision* (Chicago, 1971); Stella P. Revard, *The War in Heaven: Paradise Lost and the Tradition of Satan's Rebellion* (Ithaca, NY, 1980); and David Loewenstein, *Milton and the Drama of History: Historical Vision,*

Iconoclasm, and the Literary Imagination (Cambridge, 1990), on the final books of the epic. Among useful collections of modern essays are the following: *Milton: Paradise Lost*, ed. Louis L. Martz (Englewood Cliffs, NJ, 1966); *Approaches to Paradise Lost*, ed. C. A. Patrides (Toronto, 1968); *New Essays on Paradise Lost*, ed. Thomas Kranidas (Berkeley, 1969); *Paradise Lost: A Tercentenary Tribute*, ed. Balachandra Rajan (Toronto, 1969); *Paradise Lost: A Casebook*, ed. A. E. Dyson and Julian Lovelock (London, 1973). *Re-membering Milton: Essays on the Texts and Traditions*, ed. Mary Nyquist and Margaret W. Ferguson (London, 1988), is a stimulating collection of theoretically engaged essays written from diverse critical perspectives. Some of the more recent critical approaches to the poet may also be sampled in *John Milton*, ed. Annabel Patterson (London and New York, 1992) and *Critical Essays on John Milton*, ed. Christopher Kendrick (New York, 1995).

Literary after-life

In *Regaining Paradise: Milton and the Eighteenth-Century* (Cambridge, 1986), Dustin Griffin considers the responses of Restoration and eighteenth-century writers and dissents from Bloom's argument (see below) that Milton was an intimidating influence. Griffin's study is now supplemented by Leslie E. Moore, *Beautiful Sublime: The Making of Paradise Lost, 1701–1734* (Stanford, 1990). For Romantic responses, see *The Romantics on Milton: Formal Essays and Critical Asides*, ed. Joseph A. Wittreich (Cleveland, 1970), a generous collection of primary materials. Important studies of Romantic responses include: Herbert Grierson, *Milton and Wordsworth* (Cambridge, 1937); Harold Bloom, *The Anxiety of Influence* (New York, 1973); Leslie Brisman, *Milton's Poetry of Choice and Its Romantic Heirs* (Ithaca, NY, 1973); *Milton and the Line of Vision*, ed. Joseph A. Wittreich (Madison, 1975); and Lucy Newlyn, *Paradise Lost and the Romantic Reader* (Oxford, 1993). The poem's considerable influence is also the subject of R. D. Havens, *The Influence of Milton on English Poetry* (Cambridge, MA, 1922). *Milton [1628–1731]: The Critical Heritage* (London, 1970) and *Milton, 1732–1801: The Critical Heritage* (London, 1972), both edited by J. T. Shawcross, are valuable for the history of critical commentary. Joseph Wittreich's *Feminist Milton* (Ithaca, NY, 1987) studies the later responses of women readers. On Milton's reception in other periods, see George Sensabaugh, *Milton and Early America* (Princeton, 1964); Robin Grey, *The Complicity of Imagination: The American Renaissance, Contests of Authority, and Seventeenth-Century English Culture* (Cambridge, 1997); James G. Nelson, *The Sublime Puritan: Milton and the Victorians* (Madison, 1963); and Patrick Murray, *Milton: The Modern Phase* (London, 1967).